POR

POUSA

STUART ROSS

Fifth edition, wholly revised, 2001
First published, 1986.
Second edition, 1992.
Third edition, 1994.
Fourth edition, 1998.
Text copyright: Stuart Ross.
Illustrations: Most area photos by Marion Kaplan.
Most pousada photos by Enatur.
Other photos by Stuart Ross, Len Port and Peter Daughtrey.

Published by Vista Ibérica Publicações, Lda.
Len Port (Editor), Peter Daughtrey (Designer),
No. Contribuinte 504 788 671
Urbanização Lagoa-Sol - Lote 1B - 8400-415 Lagoa
Tel: (+351) 282 340 660
Fax: (+351) 282 343 088
E-mail: vistaiberica@mail.telepac.pt

Printed by Litográfica do Sul, S.A., V.R. de Santo António

ISBN: 972-8044-32-1
Depósito Legal No. 124062/98

Contents

The Province of Algarve

"there is a great deal more to the Algarve than the pleasure beaches, golf courses and yachting marinas..."

Together with the Minho in the extreme north, the Algarve is the smallest province in Portugal. It is only one-fifth the size of the adjoining province of Alentejo and yet it is probably the best known area in the country. The international airport at its capital, Faro, brings holidaymakers in their thousands to its superb beaches, golf courses, villas and hotels. With over 3,000 sun hours per annum it is no surprise that this most southern of the provinces has become one of the great playgrounds of Europe. Sheltered from the north by mountain ranges and tempered in the south by its nearness to Africa, the climate is as good as Europe has to offer. No wonder then that the beaches and golf courses along its 130 mile coastline are increasingly popular. All this development has taken place in a relatively short time.

Until the 1950's, the Algarve was the best kept secret in Europe. A few wealthy Lisbon families had summer residences overlooking the sea and there were a handful of small but charming hotels, like the Bela Vista at Praia da Rocha which, much extended and modernised, still exists today.

When we first purchased a property at Praia do Carvoeiro in 1963, there was no airport in the Algarve so we flew from London to Gibraltar, hired a car, motored via Seville to the Guadiana river on the eastern border of Portugal, and crossed by car ferry from Ayamonte in Spain to Vila Real de Santo António. At that time we had one of the three telephones in our

Opposite top: Ferragudo
Opposite: Praia D. Ana
This page, from top: Quinta do Lago,
February blossoms, Vila Real de St° António,
Carvoeiro, Monchique.

neighbourhood; now there are over 2,000!

By the end of the '60s, access to the Algarve had improved. The airport at Faro had been completed and a handsome new bridge spanned the sheltered waters of the Tagus at Lisbon. Previously, apart from the ferry, there was only a road crossing at Villa Franca de Xira, some 20 miles upstream from Lisbon. With improved communications, coastal development started in a big way. Multinational companies erected vast hotels; villas proliferated. The donkey gave way to the motorbike and the car as a means of travel. The Algarve was on the foreigners' itinerary. It featured in package tour brochures. The English were the first of the continental countries to invade its beaches and its increasing number of golf courses. So much so that I recall a cartoon in a Portuguese national newspaper - it must have been in the early '70s - in which a Lisbon youth asked

his father if the family could holiday in the Algarve. "No," replied the father, "it's no good going there - we don't speak English."

The English can claim a far more significant and materially older link with the Algarve. Edward III's granddaughter married the King of Portugal. Their son, Prince Henry, turned out to be one of the great brains of the 15th century. Obsessed with what lay beyond this most southwesterly part of Europe, he set up a school near Sagres to study navigation. His pioneering work brought Africa, India and the New World on to our atlases where before there had been darkness, ignorance and rumour.

A long time before the English could claim any link with the Algarve, the Phoenicians, Greeks, Romans and more particularly the Moors had left indelible marks on both the people and the landscape. The name 'Algarve' is from the Arabic *Al-Gharb* - meaning 'the west' - and the 500-year Moorish occupation is responsible for much that we take for granted today. They planted fig, almond, orange and lemon trees and introduced courtyards, terracotta tiles and weaving. They also instilled an eastern dark-skinned beauty into the faces and figures of many Algarvians.

There is a good deal more to the Algarve than the pleasure beaches, golf courses and yachting marinas. Find time if you can to explore the hinterland. Wander round the old Moorish capital of Silves, tramp over the mountains beyond Monchique and sample the waters of the nearby spa. Motor over to the Guadiana and follow the river

from the fortified town of Castro Marim to Alcoutim. If you want to know more, Len Port's *Get to know the Algarve* is compulsive reading. There is even an abridged pocket edition, *Algarve in your Pocket.**

Whereas so much that goes on in the Algarve today is geared to the tourist trade, one must not forget that the ancient fishing industry was established well before the first golf course was laid out, or the first  foreigner set foot on its beaches. The trawlers bring their catches daily to the markets along the coast. Fish from the markets of Portimão, Lagos, Albufeira, Olhão and Faro taste of the sea. They could not be fresher and the waterside fish restaurants do a roaring trade with visitors who hitherto have only tasted fish fighting hard to beat their sell-by date at the local supermarket. Cork, fir and eucalyptus provide an extensive timber trade and are grown inland, particularly in the Monchique mountains where the scent of wood smoke often mingles with the aroma of chicken piri-piri, a spicy barbecued speciality. Also from these parts you may sample locally produced honey and *medronho*, a pretty powerful aqua vitae.

ENATUR, who are responsible for the development of the pousada chain, have restricted their presence in Algarve to Sagres and São Brás de Alportel, although more are in prospect.

In brief, Algarve is to Portugal what California and the Côte d'Azur are to America and France. Algarve is cheaper and lovelier. It is much better planned and far more attractive than its near rival, southern Spain.

* Both books are published by Vista Ibérica Publicações.

Opposite left: Praia do Vau
Opposite bottom: Caldas de Monchique
Right: Cape St. Vicent - Sagres
Below: Guadiana River

T his pousada was one of two purpose-built government projects in 1942. It has received several major face-lifts since and it is hard to visualise the original plebeian structure. Now complete with swimming pool and tennis court, it has everything the holidaymaker could wish. Thirty-five minutes drive from the coast, it is well-removed from the hurly-burly of the resorts and yet it is accessible both to the beaches and golf courses. Here you get the best of two

worlds, for the Algarve is a province of contrasts, from the coastal plains to magnificent mountain scenery, from parched lowlands to the fast flowing streams and even waterfalls of the hinterland. It is a region of quaint chimneys and of traditional crafts and customs, of almond blossom and eucalyptus trees, of mimosa and cork, of palms and firs and kind, gentle people who, even if they do not understand you, convey by look or a smile a welcoming friendship.

Do not leave these parts without a visit to Faro. Many visitors are only acquainted with the airport, but the town has a good shopping centre with many roads

> *here you get the best of two worlds, for the Algarve is a province of contrasts*

R

33

confined to pedestrians. The guidebooks tell you what to see but may overlook a couple of gems. Alongside the cathedral is the macabre chapel of bones. Built entirely of skeletons of exhumed monks, it bears the timely reminder: "these bones are waiting for yours". We also have a former convent nearby to thank for a true Thespian jewel, the Teatro Lethes. It was erected by an Italian, Dr Lazaro Doglioni, in the 1800s and it is an exquisite small-scale La Scala. During the annual Algarve Music Festival, from the end of April to the beginning of July, you may be lucky enough to see a performance here.

Estói with its 18th-century 'palace', the former home of the Counts of Carvalhal, is a pleasant and worthwhile run. Loulé (13 kms on N270) is a sizeable and expanding market town. It has a Moorish atmosphere which is apparent in the market building. Although the construction is relatively modern, it recalls Córdoba or the Alcazar in Seville. If you take the road north from the pousada via Alportel, just south of Barranco do Velho the N124 to your left runs more or less parallel with the much busier coast road. It passes through Alte (worth a stop to see the fountain and grottoes), S. Bartolomeu de Messines, and on to Silves where the old castle provides some shady gardens and ramparts overlooking the river Arade.

It is hard to imagine anything more restful and peaceful than the pousada at São Brás de Alportel. Incidentally, *al portel* is Moorish for 'the gateway'. Those who pass through its entrance will not forget or regret it.

POUSADA ACTIVITIES

Swimming pool, family games and tennis.

AREA ACTIVITIES

Golf, water sports, canoeing, cruises (river), horse riding, four-wheel driving, mountain cycling, shooting, gymnasium, paintball and karting.

HOW TO FIND

Fairly easy. S. Brás is 30kms north of Faro (on the Algarve coast). Take the main Lisbon road from S. Brás. After 2kms there is a small road off to the right which goes to the pousada.

increasing numbers of visitors want to see the most southwesterly corner of Europe and learn about the man who gave his name to the pousada

This purpose-built pousada has a superb position on the cliff-top overlooking Sagres fort and the lighthouse of Cape St Vincent, off which many great sea battles have been fought by the likes of Admirals Drake, Rodney, Nelson and Napier. Since its erection in 1960, the pousada has been constantly improved to cater for the increasing number of visitors who want to see this most southwesterly corner of Europe and to learn something of the history of the man who gave his name to the pousada. *Infante D. Henrique* is Portuguese for Prince Henry, the son of King João I and his English-born queen Philippa of Lancaster, who founded a navigation school here early in the 15th century. As you sip your Sagres beer on the terrace, remember Prince Henry planned expeditions which prodded and probed their way down the west coast of Africa and then, via the Azores and Madeira, to the New World. His fleets reached India and it is no coincidence that Bombay is so named. It is a corruption of the Portuguese *boa baía* (good bay). Goa, which has beaches to rival Portugal's, remained Portuguese territory until 1961. Even Christopher Colombus had the good sense to marry a Portuguese girl and do some of his navigational training at Sagres. It is a tragedy that more is not made of this cornerstone of history when Portugal was at its zenith. Someone with the imagination of a Prince Henry the Navigator is badly needed to create displays to explain the 15th-century achievements of this great maritime nation. There used to be a little cinema which made some attempt to paint a picture

POUSADA DE SAGRES

Infante

R

39

POUSADA ACTIVITIES

Swimming pool, tennis and snooker.

AREA ACTIVITIES

Golf, horse riding, diving, handgliding, mountain bikes, water sports, country walks, fishing and deep sea fishing, cruises, four-wheel driving and Water Parks.

HOW TO FIND

Easy. In the town itself, on the coast.

of the past. Since this shut down, street vendors now have pride of place on a historic site which promises so much and achieves so little.

Like many promontories in the southwest of other European countries, Sagres is shaven by the prevailing wind. It is bare, blustery and bleak; yet it has a strange, severe and haunting beauty. In the calm summer months, the stillness, tranquillity and the friendly sparkling sea are but a welcome interlude before the winter winds whistle across the empty plains, and the snarling seas thrash against giant cliffs with an awe inspiring ferocity. Spume is flung high into the lowering sky and shipping keeps well off the point.

There are several sheltered sandy beaches. Birdwatching, wind-surfing and fishing are popular local pastimes. Have a look at Lagos (33 kms). It is a port with a new marina, but way back in history many of Prince Henry's early caravels were built here. His statue stands in the square where the well-preserved *Mercado dos Escravos* (slave market) is a timely reminder that not only gold, ivory and spices were brought back from those newly-found lands across the seas.

The efficiency and friendliness of this modern pousada compensate for the disappointments of the Infante's 'navigation school'. If you wish to arrive in style, there is now a heliport.

The Fortaleza do Beliche, on the road to the lighthouse, is run by the pousada as an annexe. It has a small, attractive restaurant and a 17th century chapel. It makes a delightful stop for a drink, lunch or dinner. It also has the attraction of providing four bedrooms in this ancient and commandingly scenic spot.

Index

Mesão Frio	Solar da Rede	60	Tel: 254 89 01 30 Fax:254 89 01 39
M. do Douro	Santa Catarina	50	Tel: 273 43 12 55/005 Fax:273 43 10 65
Monsanto	Monsanto	84	Tel: 277 31 44 71/2/3 Fax:277 31 44 81
Óbidos	Castelo	100	Tel: 262 95 91 05/46 Fax:262 95 91 48
Ourém	Conde de Ourém	88	Tel: 249 54 09 20 Fax:249 54 29 55
Palmela	Castelo de Palmela	104	Tel: 21 235 12 26 Fax:21 233 04 40
P. das Quartas	Santa Bárbara	76	Tel: 238 60 95 51/3/652 Fax:238 60 96 45
Queluz	D. Maria I	102	Tel: 21 435 61 58/72/81 Fax:21 435 61 89
Sagres	Infante	160	Tel: 282 62 42 22/3 Fax:282 62 42 25
S.Clara-a-Velha	Santa Clara	148	Tel: 283 88 22 50/48/404 Fax:283 88 24 02
S. do Cacém	São Tiago	144	Tel: 269 82 24 59/69 Fax:269 82 24 59
S. do Cacém	Quinta da Ortiga	146	Tel: 269 82 28 71/0 74 Fax:269 82 20 73
S. B. de Alportel	São Brás	158	Tel: 289 84 23 05/6 Fax:289 84 17 26
Serpa	São Gens	152	Tel: 284 54 47 24/5 Fax:284 54 43 37
Setúbal	São Filipe	108	Tel: 265 52 38 44/49 81 Fax:265 53 25 38
Sousel	São Miguel	120	Tel: 268 55 00 50 Fax:268 55 11 55
Tomar	São Pedro	90	Tel: 249 38 11 59/75 Fax:249 38 11 76
Torrão	Vale do Gaio	140	Tel: 265 66 96 10/97 97 Fax:265 66 95 45
Torreira	Ria	68	Tel: 234 86 01 80 Fax:234 83 83 33
Valença do Minho	São Teotónio	32	Tel: 251 82 42 42/52/020 Fax:251 82 43 97
Viana do Castelo	Monte Sta. Luzia	28	Tel: 258 82 88 89/90/1 Fax:258 82 88 92
V. N. de Cerveira	D. Diniz	30	Tel: 251 70 81 20 Fax:251 70 81 29
Vila Viçosa	D. João IV	132	Tel: 268 98 07 42/3/4/5 Fax:268 98 07 47

Preface

When I prepared the first edition of this book thirteen years ago I thought and hoped it would fill a need among those travellers who, like me, were sometimes sceptical of publicity-orientated leaflets from tourist offices, which were as quick to extol the virtues as they were slow to stress the drawbacks. In travelling around Portugal, particularly in a limited holiday period, one cannot affort to make too many mistakes and I wanted to help in planning an itinerary and avoiding the difficulties, disappointments and frustrations I had sometimes experienced.

The fact that I am now rewriting PORTUGAL'S POUSADA ROUTE for the fifth time confirms my original belief. I only hope I do the subject justice.

Thirteen years ago there were 30 pousadas. Today there are 45. The increase in numbers has both added to the choice of the type of pousada, and of the area you might wish to explore. Since the first edition in 1986 there have been substantial improvements not only in the pousadas themselves, but in the road network throughout the country. Standards of service and food are much higher; so are prices - but the increases are no greater than in other European countries and still represent good value for money. I have tried to give an unbiased opinion of what is good, both with each pousada and the area in which it is located.

It has been decided, in an effort to make the guide more user-friendly and to facilitate the location of the increasing number of pousadas, to divide the country into its historical provinces.

Hopefully this will also make it easier to plan your itinerary and to explore a particular region.

Wherever possible I have consulted other guests in an endeavour to reach a fair conclusion. Individual opinions varied from the over-enthusiastic to the destructively cynical. I have tried to adopt an independent middle course and to provide information concerning each pousada which may add to the pleasure at your stay.

In times of rapidly changing political, social and economic conditions it would be surprising if the opinions expressed here were not similarly subject to revision in some cases. The management and staff of pousadas change. Standards change. Telephone numbers are for ever changing. Even from friends whose opinions I respect, I have received contradictory reports on meals at the same pousada.

Every care has been taken to avoid inaccuracies and errors, but it is difficult to ensure none occurs.

That fact that I greatly enjoyed revisiting the pousadas and writing this fifth edition

is due in part, as I have said, to the improved conditions and to the help I received from many people who made time to see me, answer my questions and point me in the direction of interesting avenues of enquiry. I am particularly grateful to ENATUR (Pousadas de Portugal) and those who accompanied me throughout the tour.

Finally thank you Portugal for being such a lovely and hospitable country.

STUART ROSS
(Serra de Monchique)

Pousada Prelude

THE BEGINNING

The word *pousada* comes from the Portuguese verb *pousar*, which the dictionary translates as 'to lay down a burden, to lodge at, to repose.'

The pousadas form a network of government-owned hostelries and were the brainchild of Senhor António Ferro, Minister of Information and Propaganda in the 1940s. His idea was to create small regional establishments where guests would be looked after in much the same way as earlier pilgrims and travellers had received hospitality. As Sr. Ferro put it, "when a customer ceases to be called by his own name and is known merely by his room number, we will have lost entirely the spirit of the pousada."

The pousada of Santa Luzia in Elvas was the first to be opened on 19th April 1942.

THE EXPANDING NETWORK

From this simple beginning the network has expanded to cover the whole country. Today there are 45 pousadas, all ensuring a high standard of comfort. Many are located in former castles, convents, monasteries and buildings of historic interest. Others have been chosen for their exceptional situations overlooking lakes or scenery of outstanding beauty. They range from the relatively simple to the opulent, and they all provide an opportunity to acquire a knowledge of the culture, customs and cuisine of the various regions.

The larger the growth in the number of pousadas the more difficult it becomes to preserve the spirit of the original conception. The fact that there is considerable autonomy in each of the pousadas greatly adds to their individuality and character and helps to avoid the faceless, soulless state-run atmosphere at one time prevalent in Spain, for example.

ENATUR, the company which operate the pousadas, has simplified its earlier grading system and now categorise each as either 'historical' or 'regional.' To avoid confusion, we have adopted the same categories. An information panel for each pousada in the pages that follow, also gives details of the number of rooms, amenities

and activities, and directions on how to get there.

Incidentally, none of the pousadas admit dogs.

PRICES AND PAYMENT

For pricing purposes, the year is divided into two seasons, not three as before:

· **Low** - 1st November to 31st March (except New Year and Carnival when higher rates apply).

· **High** - 1st April to 31st October.

It has been recent practice to make a 50% reduction in some pousadas for visitors over 60 years of age (foreign as well as Portuguese) during the low season. This offer excludes weekends and national holidays, but it is a very substantial saving in accommodation costs with breakfast (other meals are excluded). Only one of a couple needs to have reached the *Idade de ouro* (Golden Age). Enquire when booking whether this concession applies. It is for you to decide whether you are prepared to gamble on the weather.

All of the pousadas accept credit cards. A service charge is included in meal bills, but it is surprising how often an extra tip for friendly and helpful service is more than warranted.

RESERVATIONS

It is as well to remember that the number of tourists visiting Portugal approaches 10 million each year and that the demand for accommodation, particularly in high season, often exceeds supply. Book as early as you can to avoid disappointment. There is no limit to the length of stay but in practice, owing to the demand in high season, accommodation in some pousadas will be extremely difficult to obtain without prior reservation. If your itinerary has not been arranged before departure, the pousada where you are staying can be very helpful in arranging subsequent accommodation.

The central reservations office is in Lisbon.

· Telephone: 00 351 218 442 001
· Fax: 00 351 218 442 085
· E-mail: guest@pousadas.pt
· Website: www.pousadas.pt

POUSADA TIMES

You may arrive earlier but, unless prior payment has been made, not later than the stipulated time (usually between 1800 and 2000 hrs). The same applies to checking out, which varies between 0800 and 1000 hrs. Rooms should be vacated by midday.

Restaurant times are now the same in all pousadas. Meals are as follows: breakfast 0730-1000, available in your bedroom without extra charge; lunch 1230-1500; dinner 1930-2200.

The Portuguese operate a 24-hour clock and find our 12-hour clock just as confusing as some visitors find the 24-hour method. Don't be surprised, therefore, to discover you may have dinner "until 2200am". Anyway, on holiday, a glass of port at 2200am is as good a time as any!

TRAVEL TIPS

Despite the risk of rain, there is much to be said for low season travel. The centre of Portugal can be uncomfortably hot in the height of the summer with temperatures of 37ºC (98º Fahrenheit) quite common. An air-conditioned car is a worthwhile extravagance in July and August. The weather apart, the majority of Portuguese seem to favour August as the holiday month. Statistically it is a fact that the standard of driving is lower in Portugal than elsewhere in Europe. This is another reason for avoiding the busy hot months.

The reference to road numbers and distances in this book relate to the Michelin Map of Portugal, or *Mapa das Estradas* issued by the Automóvel Clube de Portugal. Another useful map is *Turinta,* which includes places of historical interest and a guide to restaurants, bars, etc. ENATUR sell a special edition of this map.

In the past, some of the pousadas were difficult to find, but hundreds of signs like the one illustrated on page 162 have been erected. Combined with our instructions, they should enable you to reach your destination without trouble.

In Portugal you need to carry your driving licence and passport (or certified copies) with you in the car at all times.

Food and wine

In earlier editions of *Portugal's Pousada Route* recommendations for both food and wine were given in the chapters on individual pousadas. Several readers have expressed their disappointment that the 'pheasant and red Periquita', whose virtues I had extolled, were not available when they arrived expectantly at their destination. We live in a rapidly changing world and it is no surprise to find that today's speciality is tomorrow's memory. With the ever-increasing number of pousadas, changes in management and chefs are to be expected. With these changes come new ideas on what food to offer and what wines to stock and I realise now that my comments under individual pousadas could be misleading and disappointing. It has, therefore, been decided to offer general rather than specific advice.

In the past, pousada food has not always matched up to the beautiful surroundings and buildings. In recent years, there has been much greater supervision from Lisbon-based ENATUR, which has the overall responsibility for developing and running this substantial chain of government-owned hotels. The result has been a considerable improvement in standards, both in consistency and presentation. Visitors' comments (sometimes critical) have also served to increase awareness of the need to provide the very best of food and wine.

The first and essential advice I can offer is to ask. Menus are now printed in several languages so there should be no difficulty in understanding what is available, but a word with the waiter can often elicit an idea you hadn't considered and a dish you would have been reluctant to try.

Portuguese food, like the country, is very varied and each region has its specialities. With increasing travel and movement of population, it is common to find what was a speciality of the north, is now readily available in the south and vice versa. *Caldo Verde*, for example, is most closely associated with the Minho area in the far northwest, but it is now available everywhere, including in the southernmost province of Algarve. Similarly, the popularity of *chicken piri-piri* from the mountains of the Algarve has spread northwards right up to Trás os Montes.

No one is better at making soups than the Portuguese. The now ubiquitous *Caldo Verde* is a cabbage and potato soup in which the cabbage is painstakingly shredded very finely and a slice of spiced sausage often added for a final touch of flavour. *Açordas* are bread-porridge like soups flavoured with fish, meat, bacon or eggs. They are almost meals in themselves. Hot *Açordas* are winter favourites just as tomato, pepper and cucumber-based *Gaspacho* is served cold in summer. Vegetable soups come in many forms, including *Sopa de Agriões* (watercress). Fish soups are popular and probably top of the list is *Caldeirada*, actually more of a stew than a soup, which has many local variations. Similar to a bouillabaisse, *Caldeirada* is made from a variety of filleted fish, such as bass, hake, skate and whitebait, plus a mixture of shellfish, usually including cockles, mussels, and shrimps.

Cataplana is a uniquely Portuguese seafood dish, which takes its name from the twin, tight-fitting dishes it is cooked in. It is a sort of primitive pressure cooker made of aluminum or copper. *Cataplana* ingredients - usually fish, shellfish, pork or sausages - are steamed in their own juices. *Amêijoas e porco na Cataplana* (cockles and pork) is a favourite in the Algarve. The Portuguese are good at mixing the flavour of fish with meat. Trout stuffed with ham is popular in the Douro and Minho regions.

Arroz de marisco (shellfish rice) is a very tasty dish and a half portion can make a good start to the meal. While some of the shellfish are improved with improvisation, there are a number of reliable white fish that do not require embellishment. As you would expect in a country whose entire coastline is bounded by the Atlantic Ocean, fish in Portugal is superb - different again from the fish netted in the polluted

waters of the Mediterranean. *Cherne, robalo, pargo and linguado* (halibut, sea bass, snapper and sole) are all excellent. Sardines are still beloved by the Portuguese, though only really at their best in the summer months. Barbequed with a hunk of fresh bread, fresh sardines rival any of their more expensive cohabitants of the deep.

It would be sacrilege to return to your native hearth without experimenting with *bacalhau*, which is cod, but probably very different to the cod you are used to. Traditionally caught by Portuguese fishermen as far away as the banks of Newfoundland, *bacalhau* is cod that has been dried and salted. This custom started in the days before refrigeration when drying and salting was the only method of preserving fish during the long sea voyages to discover foreign shores. *Bacalhau*, which needs to be well soaked in water before cooking, may sound uninspiring, but the Portuguese are passionate about it, so much so that there are said to be 365 recipes - one for each day of the year. Our favourites are *Bacalhau á Brás* and *Bacalhau á Gomes de Sá*, both of which are cooked with potatoes, onion and egg; *Bacalhau com natas* is cooked in a cream sauce; in *Bacalhau gratinado*, the cod and potatoes are baked in béchamel sauce and topped with cheese. If you are unsure you will like it enough to order a main course, one portion between two makes an interesting starter.

The standard of meat has improved enormously during my time in Portugal. It was often not hung for a sufficient length of time and could be very tough. Pork is the most widely eaten meat, followed by chicken. The *lombo* is the fillet of pork and in *Lombo assado à Alentejana* it is roasted in a white wine sauce. Chicken casseroled in a deep earthenware pot with mustard, brandy, port and seasonings appears on the menu as well-loved *Frango na Púcara*. Lamb is not much eaten, though *cabrito* (kid) can be flavoursome. I would still be wary of steak, though if you hanker after it, insist on fillet or it is likely to be very chewy. *Javali* (wild boar) appears on pousada menus from time to time - give it a go; accompanied by a good red wine, I would be astounded if you don't like it. Partridge, pheasant, guinea fowl and rabbit all appear in season and are recommended if you are in hunting territory.

To round off a meal there is a wide range of cheese, each pousada stocking its individual choice. Cheddar-like cheese from the islands of the Azores is among the best, but so are the soft cheeses from Serra da Estrela in the north.

Fresh fruits, such as oranges and figs, are plentiful; so too are the soft fruits. You will often find pineapples on the menu; they are imports from São Miguel in the Azores.

Many pousadas have exceptional pastry cooks and some of the sweets they produce make one regret previous gluttony. Almond cake, the erogenous and syrupy *Papos de Anjo* (angels' breasts), Amarante's *Bolinho do Amor* (love cake), light, fluffy molotov puddings and mixtures of chestnut and chocolate are banquets in themselves.

Commenting on the wines of Portugal is no easy task in a limited space, for Portugal is the seventh largest wine-producing country in the world and it has an immense range to choose from. Increasingly, Portuguese wines are being given the recognition they deserve abroad. In recent years they have been showered with medals in competitions in France and London. When in Portugal, drink Portuguese. Don't even think about French or any other. Portugal produces all types of wine - apertifs, *vinhos verdes* and sparkling wines in the north; white and red table wines in north, centre and south; dessert wines in Setúbal and Madeira, as well the world-famous Douro region. The Portuguese love of making wine is only matched by their love of drinking it. Dry reds and whites are consumed in such quantity at home that

it is no wonder so little is available abroad.

Young foward-looking wine-makers using the great variety of indigenous grapes are producing some superb wines and the wine world is becoming very excited about new wines being made from single grape varieties unique to Portugal.

One result of increased central control by ENATUR is the purchase of wines in bulk and you will find them on the wine list under *Adega Pousadas de Portugal*. One advantage of this standardisation is that having found a wine that you really like, you are confident it will be available at your next pousada, while still allowing you to experiment if you wish. The more adventurous, however, will be pleased to know that individual pousada directors may supplement the standard list with their own selection of regional wines.

Dry white port is a first-rate aperitif and Portuguese champagne-style wine is a good substitute for the Champagne of France at a fraction of the cost. *Vinhos verdes* (green wines) are either red or more commonly white in colour and are called 'green' only because they are young. For anyone who has managed to get through life so far without tasting Mateus Rosé, the most appropriate place to put that right is in Amarante in the Douro Litoral where it is made. One wine critic wrote that to enjoy Mateus Rosé you had either to be mad or a shareholder! Don't you believe it - a glass of Mateus Rosé with a gooey cake at about eleven o'clock is good for the soul if not the waistline.

Astride the main north-south road between Oporto and Coimbra in the province of Beira is the home of Bairrada, in our opinion some of the best table wines Portugal has to offer. Among the many reliable names to look for are Aliança, Frei João, Sogrape and Luis Pato.

Although far less known outside of Portugal, the wines of the Alentejo run a very close second to Bairradas. They are excellent value. Redondo, Vidigueira, Reguengos, Esporão and Borba are all from the Alentejo and it is not necessary to look further afield as they are all available in both red and white. Offhand, I cannot recall a poor one.

It is difficult to go wrong with wines from the wild and hilly Dão region. Dao's outstanding reputation is founded on its reds, but it also produces good whites. The Dãos are a good accompaniment to any meal and are available all over the country.

We have always been disappointed with the wines of the Algarve. Although improving, the local offerings from Lagoa and Lagos still have a long way to go. Elsewhere, though, in the Ribatejo and Estremadura regions for example,

local wines can be excellent. The Palmela - Setúbal area south of Lisbon is now producing some outstanding wines.

The hieroglyphics on wine labels may puzzle and interest you. D.O.C. (*Denominação de Origem Controlada*) is wine of a designated area. I.P.R. (*Indicação de Proveniência Regulamentada*) is much the same as D.O.C. in a region not formally demarcated by the government. V.Q.P.R.D. (*Vinho de Qualidade Produzido em Região Determinada*) is a quality wine approved by the Wine Commission. *Garrafeira* refers to up-market red wines of quality with long bottle maturity. They can be expensive, but worth it if you have the money and wish to spend some of it on wine.

How can we leave a chapter on food and wine without mention of Port? It is hopeless to try to summarise Port in a few words: books have been written on the subject. The pousada Port is very drinkable at a reasonable price, but if you get interested in the subject and want to know more, the wine is extremely well promoted and marketed. You can visit any of the major producers' warehouses at Vila Nova de Gaia where illustrated lectures and tastings are arranged. Better still, stay in either the Alijó or Mesão Frio pousadas. The Douro provides magnificent scenery in addition to the universally known port wine.

Page 12: Regional dishes
Pages 13, 14, 15: Pousadas
restaurants.
Page 16: Molotov pudding.
Above: Cataplana.
Right: Algarve almond confections.

Tours & Touring

Unless you have an air-conditioned car, our advice would be to keep away from the southern half of the country in the last week of July, August and the first week of September. The north of Portugal is cooler than the south and freezing conditions may be met in the Serra da Estrela and the highlands of Trás-os-Montes during the winter months. The wettest months are November and December. During the other winter months there is often rain interspersed with sun and blue skies. The climate sometimes changes very quickly and a ghastly damp, dull day in winter can be followed by spring-like weather.

Portugal is not a very big country, but if some of the places mentioned in each chapter are to be explored without a mad rush, the country divides itself into two halves. Roughly, the dividing line connects the pousadas of Batalha, Ourém, Castelo de Bode (Tomar) and Marvão. North of this line there are 20 pousadas and south of it there is a corresponding number making a total at present of 44. Others, like Tavira in Algarve are planned, and may be available by the time of your arrival. Also, in the southern half, of course, is Lisbon which is one of the loveliest capitals in Europe. It would be a great pity to miss it when doing the southern tour. Sadly, as yet there is no pousada in the centre of the capital, but there is a good selection of hotels. The pousada at Queluz (13 kms) can also make a relaxing headquarters from which to explore both the city, Queluz Palace and surrounding places of interest (Sintra and Ajuda, etc.).

NORTHERN TOUR

On a fly/drive visit, Oporto is a good starting point. If you are driving your own car, there are many frontier points of entry, either across the river Minho in the extreme north or on the eastern boundary with Spain, including the major one at

Vilar Formoso. The merits of nearby Almeida as a place to unwind are mentioned under the Chapter on Senhora das Neves. This could be followed by some mountain scenery at Manteigas, then Oliveira do Hospital and on the Serem. If you fancy a seaside stop, Viana do Castelo would be a good choice. Inland, some interesting scenery would enable you to visit Santa Maria do Bouro. Head up north to the border town of Valença or Vila Nova de Cerveira, south to the mountain retreat of Caniçada, south again to Guimarães (two pousadas to choose from), across country to Alijó to learn all about port wine, before making for the outpost of Miranda do Douro. This involves a minimum of 10 pousadas. Two nights in each, or certainly in some of them, and perhaps one in Oporto (where the stock exchange must not be missed) and all too quickly a three-week holiday has disappeared. This is why it is best to have two bites at the cherry by coming back next year and taking a more southerly route.

SOUTHERN TOUR

A fly/drive tour would start either at Lisbon or Faro. Arriving by road, there are several frontier crossings along Portugal's eastern border, the main three being on the road to Elvas from Badajoz, the road to Serpa from Aracena, and - the most southerly - either by ferry or the new bridge at Vila Real de Santo António.

The point of arrival will decide the sequence of visits. Clockwise from Faro we suggest São Brás de Alportel as a good stop to 'get the feel of things' and relax before moving on to Sagres. Travel north to Santiago de Cacém and north again to either Setúbal or Palmela. Take the motorway over the Tagus Bridge to Lisbon, which warrants two nights. Drive across country to the three 'E's - Évora, Estremoz and Elvas though miss the last one unless you are arriving or leaving by this frontier crossing and include instead Vila Viçosa or Arraiolos. Head south now through the heart of Alentejo to Serpa and then south again to Faro with perhaps another night en route at São Brás.

CENTRAL TOUR

It will be noted that the central dividing line of pousadas has not been included in either of the above itineraries. Once again it is a question of time. Time permitting, they can be incorporated in either one or other of the tours suggested above. In point of fact they make a very natural visit on their own. This is because a central tour should include Lisbon, Alcobaça, Batalha and Tomar all of them absolute MUSTS but nevertheless time consuming if they are to be appreciated to the full. A suggestion for the fly/driver starting from Lisbon would be two nights in the capital; then Óbidos (just south of Caldas da Rainha on the map); north-east to Batalha, stopping on the way to look at Alcobaça, east after Batalha to Ourém or Tomar (Castelo de Bode) passing Fátima en route, and east again to Marvão. Nearby Castelo de Vide is interesting and a convenient spot to turn south for the two lovely Alentejo pousadas at Estremoz and Évora. Thence, sadly, back to Lisbon and the plane home.

IN GENERAL

Portuguese and foreign residents in Portugal have the opportunity to enjoy the countryside as and when opportunity and the desire strike. A weekend´s skiing is not an impossibility when conditions are right. For those lucky enough to live permanently in Portugal, this book will, hopefully, encourage visits to less familiar parts of the country.

For the holiday visitor a massive cultural intake may call for a counterbalancing

laze. After absorbing some of the architectural and historical wonders that Portugal has to offer - and there are many, a night or two in the quiet of the countryside is a delightful way of recharging the batteries and recapturing all you have seen without the immediate pressure of absorbing more. The following come to mind as restful and relaxing by-waters and they are not too far from either Lisbon or Faro: São Brás, Alvito, Arraiolos, Santa Clara-a-Velha

and Vale do Gaio.

In the north, Mesão Frio (one of the latest to be opened) provides a very peaceful environment overlooking the lovely Douro river and valley. Similarly Ria, near Aveiro, with lagoon waters lapping the pousada's walls is another tranquil spot. Other favourites up north are Caniçada and, of course, the isolated Miranda do Douro. All these give the traveller peace and quiet in delightful surroundings.

Some visitors may prefer to see a restricted amount of Portugal from a single or perhaps a couple of pousadas. To return to a familiar base at night has its advantages. This is true if you are adverse to 'living out of a suitcase' which many claim is necessitated by visiting a series of pousadas for one night only. It depends on your individual requirement. Some wish to take every opportunity on their visit to see as much as they possibly can, others consider this secondary to their personal comfort and convenience. For many a compromise between the two is the solution. The chapter on each pousada and the text on the district or province will provide the traveller with suggestions on what to see.

You will have your own ideas on what to take with you on your trip but I have found, apart from decent maps, the following most useful: field-glasses, a bird identification book like Collins "The Birds of Britain and Europe" and if this guide is not sufficient, A. C. Black's "Blue" Guide. I have also recently treated myself to a hand-held GPS (global positioning system). Mine was made by Garmin, but there are others on the market. At the press of a button it gives, in addition to your exact latitude and longitude, your height above sea-level. It is always comforting and reassuring to know how near to heaven you are!

Make frequent stops to enjoy points of interest. Find time for a midday break for lunch, however light. It is fatal to drive all day without a stop and then tuck in to drinks and a hearty meal late at night. If you choose to ignore this advice take your favourite indigestion tablets!

Have a good trip. It is difficult not to enjoy Portugal.

General Information

Travel documents - Passports or identy cards are necessary for all foreign visitors. Visas are not needed by EC nationals, Americans, Canadians, Australians or New Zealanders.

Language - English and to a lesser extent French and German, are spoken by many of the Portuguese people with whom foreign visitors commonly come into contact in pousadas, restaurants, banks, shops and places of recreation. Language is seldom a problem, even though the majority of Portuguese speak only their mother tongue. Even in very remote areas it is not uncommon to find a German or French-speaking villager, probably on holiday or retired from employment overseas.

Pousada reservations - These may be made through ENATUR, Av. Santa Joana Princesa 10A, 1749-090 Lisboa.

Tel.: 00 351 21 844 20 00/1

Fax: 00 351 21 844 20 85/7

E-mail: guest@pousadas.pt

www.pousadas.pt

We advise making your reservation by fax. Bookings may also be made by contacting the individual Pousadas directly. If possible, bookings should be made well in advance.

Payment - Accommodation and all services at Pousadas may be paid for in cash, by travellers' cheques or by credit card.

Driving - Drive on the right. The speed limits are 50 kph (33 mph) in built-up zones, 90 kph (56 mph) on the open road and 120 kph (75 mph) on motorways. If stopped by traffic police, drivers must be able to show a valid licence, vehicle registration, insurance documents and a letter of authorisation if the vehicle is owned by other than the occupants. If you are hiring a car make sure all likely drivers are covered in the contract. In the event of an accident involving another vehicle, exchange names and addresses and insurance details. If there is serious damage or injury, the police must be informed as soon as possible. Petrol stations are scarce away from the main towns and off the main highways, so keep a careful eye on your fuel gauge.

Money - Until the Euro takes over, completely, the unit of currency is the escudo, variously written as Esc. 1, one escudo or 1$00. The numbers after the $ sign refer to centavos, now virtually worthless. The coin denominations are 1$00 (hardly used), 5$00, 10$00, 20$00, 50$00, 100$00 and 200$00. The notes are for 500, 1,000, 2,000, 5,000 and 10,000 escudos.

Banks - Exchange facilities are available at airports for all arriving and departing flights. Some, though not all, frontier posts have exchange facilities. Normal banks offering all the usual services are open from 8.30 am to 3 pm Monday to Friday; closed on weekends and public holidays. Our advice would be to obtain a nominal amount of escudos before leaving home to avoid unnecessary delay on arrival.

Postal services - Hours vary, but most of the larger post offices open from 8.30 am to 6 pm Monday to Friday. The smaller ones close for lunch. Services include international telephone and fax facilities.

Tourist offices - A great many towns frequented by visitors have a signposted *Turismo* office where English, French and German-speaking receptionists should be able to supply literature and help you with most queries. The headquarters of the National Tourist Office is at Av. António Augusto de Aguiar 86, 1069-021 Lisbon; telephone 21 358 6400; fax 21 357 5220. There are Portuguese National Tourism Offices in London, Frankfurt and throughout the world.

Electricity - The voltage is 220 AC. Appliances need two-pin plugs or adapters.

Tipping - Pousadas and most restaurants include all taxes and service charges in their bills, but in appreciation for good service a tip is in order for porters, maids and waiters. Waiters greatly appreciate a tip of 5 to 10% in addition to the service charge.

Shopping - Shops commonly close for lunch between 1 pm and 3 pm weekdays, on Saturday afternoon, all day Sunday and public holidays. Fixed prices are the norm. A certain amount of haggling goes on for such things as clothes, leather goods and other products in regional markets.

Public holidays - The main public holidays are January 1, April 25, Good Friday, May 1, Corpus Christi in June or July, June 10, August 15, October 5, November 1, December 1, December 8 and December 25. There are other local public holidays which may close offices, banks, shops, museums and monuments for the day.

Emergencies - Dial 112 anywhere in Portugal for police, fire or ambulance. Pousada reception desks and tourist information offices among other places have lists of doctors, dentists and consulates. Consulates are located in Lisbon, Oporto and Algarve. Pharmacies keep normal shop hours, but each town always has one open at night on a rota basis for prescriptions.

In Spring Portugal is awash with wild flowers.

The Minho is the most northerly of the Atlantic-facing provinces. The river Minho, which forms its northern boundary, borders Spain. In the Minho and in the adjoining province of Trás-os-Montes, the traveller always senses an atmosphere of remoteness, of strangeness, of being in foreign parts, a feeling that the people and surroundings are influenced far more by the past than by the present. The sights and sounds are from a different age. The little granaries (*espigueiros*) stand up on piles over the countryside. They look like coffins on sticks and are often surmounted by a cross which reinforces this impression. The creaking of cartwheels as oxen struggle with a challenging load is as common a sound as the rhythmic beat of a festive dance, for the people of Minho are traditionalists who know how to temper work with pleasure and have been doing so for centuries.

With an area of 4,838 sq kms, the Minho is primarily an agricultural area and the home of the best *vinho verde* (green wine), a refreshing and effervescent drink.

Braga, Viana do Castelo, Barcelos and Guimarães are the principle towns, all with ancient charm and much to offer the visitor. The province, with several interesting pousadas, provides ample accommodation from which to explore the towns and countryside. Both have much to excite the visitor. Of the towns, Guimarães is our favourite, although industrialisation spreading from nearby Vila Nova de Famalicão is a threat. Barcelos lives garishly on its cockerel legend but is still an historic town with one of Portugal's largest markets (held on Thursdays). On the coast, west of

Barcelos, Esponsende and Ofir are popular resorts, but by far the largest is Viana do Castelo at the mouth of the river Lima.

Top: Yoked oxen at work
Left: Local cheeses
Right: Peneda-Gerês
Far right top: Guimarães Castle
Far right centre: Guimarães
Far right bottom: River Minho

The Province of Minho

" the sights and sounds
are from a different age "

A number of spas dot the province, but the great national park of Peneda-Gerês - about 70.000 hectares (175,000 sq miles) - is the outstanding natural attraction of this remote area. Wild boar, wolves, wild horses and civet cats roam the deeply wooded valleys, and above the upper slopes of the Serra de Peneda great birds of prey float on thermal breezes. The park also contains a large assortment of trees and plants. Trout fishing in the Minho and its tributaries is popular and trout is often included on the menu.

Although farming in the region is, in the main, confined to small holdings

which scarcely pay their way, there are some sumptuous country houses, many around the riverside town of Ponte de Lima. The tourist office will provide details.

Local arts and crafts have survived and flourished in the Minho. Weaving, embroidery, carving, model-making, painting, ceramics and firework manufacture are all being enthusiastically carried on by families who have been doing this traditional work for very many years.

Opposite page bottom: Guimarães
Opposite page top: Braga
Below: Minho summer festival

S ince the Ancient Greeks established a trading post here, Viana do Castelo has enjoyed a cosmopolitan history. At one time the British established themselves as wine exporters, before decamping to the Douro and using Oporto for the shipment of port wine. The Jews also were merchants here. During the zenith of the Portuguese discoveries of sea routes to Asia this small fishing town became a major port rivalling the great centres of trade at Lisbon and Oporto. The ensuing wealth resulted in some handsome 16th-century building which this northern town still displays today.

It is a lovely old town on the north bank of the river Lima. In the main square (Praça da República) with its handsome fountain is where you will find some of its most attractive buildings. There are many others. The tourist office and town hall in the Palácio dos Távoras, originally the home of the Counts of Carreira, and the chapel annexed to the family home of the Malheiro Reimãos are little gems of Portuguese baroque architecture. The 18th-century home of the Barbosas Maciéis family now

> *looking down on the lovely old town, the pousada is situated in its own wooded grounds*

R

48

houses the local museum in which you can see good Indo-Portuguese furniture and decorative wall tiling. One could go on cataloguing places to see in the town, but the tourist office will provide a complete list from which you may make your own personal choice.

Looking down on the town is the Monte Santa Luzia pousada, situated in its own wooded grounds on top of a hill of the same name. Erected prior to the last World War, the hotel on four floors has been in the ownership of ENATUR for some years. After substantial works of modernisation it has been converted into a pousada. It has 48 bedrooms, the usual reception rooms, bar, terrace, swimming pool and tennis court.

Nearby are some good sandy beaches. With the amenities both of the pousada and the neighbouring town, it has proved a popular holiday venue.

HOW TO FIND

Easy. From Viana do Castelo, take the road to Santa Luzia (1km) then follow the blue signs to the pousada which is next to the Santa Luzia Monastery.

> *a fortress steeped in history, built in the late 13th or early 14th century*

Opened in 1982, this fortress pousada contains 29 spacious, air-conditioned bedrooms in three separate blocks. The bar, in what was the old prison, the breakfast room and conference room are all separately located. The dining-room is perched like a huge greenhouse on top of the ramparts with fabulous views across the Minho to Spain. The architect's intention of maintaining the personality of a garrison is clear and there is much to be said for retaining and preserving the original buildings individually.

Two little chapels, one over the entrance and one in the perimeter wall, deserve a visit - if you can get in. Secular and ecclesiastical authorities do not always combine to make access easy, but reception should be able to help.

Dom Dinis was built in the late 13th or early 14th century. It is a fortress steeped in history and it is probable that the original conception was the brainchild of Afonso III. He died in 1279 and was succeeded by Dom Dinis who finished the construction and gave the fortress its charter on 1st October 1321. Substantial changes and improvements took place in the 15th and 16th centuries. On the 25th September 1643, the garrison successfully withstood a determined attack by the Spanish.

Outside the fortress walls, the town is pleasant and expanding, with the 18th-century Igreja Matriz (parish church) not far from the pousada's entrance. In front is a memorial, dated 1809, which honours those Portuguese who gave their lives repelling a Napoleonic attack led by General Soult.

Vila Nova de Cerveira is roughly midway between Viana do Castelo and Monção. Monção is an old fortified town which has played much the same role in Portugal's history as many other frontier outposts. The town centres itself around two main squares. One of them, Praça Deu-la-Deu, is named after Senhora Deuladeu Martins. In 1368,

POUSADA DE VILA NOVA DE CERVEIRA

D. Diniz

H

29

when the town had been surrounded by the troops of Henry II of Castile, Sra Martins had the bright idea of cooking some bread and throwing it to the enemy. The invading commander thought that a garrison with so much surplus food must be so well victualled that there was no hope of surrender. He withdrew!

East of Vila Nova de Cerveira and some 8 kms this side of Melgaço (where there is a spa), a Roman bridge spans the river Mouro. History was made here. A meeting took place on Thursday 1st November 1386 between John of Gaunt (Edward III's son) and João I. The result of this meeting was the marriage the following year between John of Gaunt's daughter, Philippa of Lancaster, and King João. This was the start of the longest alliance in history.

Fishing on the Minho is a popular pastime. Trout, perch, grayling, bass and barbel are about if you are lucky. The tourist office will give you details and can often put you in touch with local anglers.

A stroll or car ride along the banks of the Minho is the real joy of staying at Dom Dinis. The fort at Lovelhe, the archaeological discoveries and the summit of Monte de Nossa Senhora da Encarnação from which a marvellous view is obtained, are all rewarding visits. Don't forget the islands of Boega, and the romantic Ilha dos Amores, which has been much photographed and painted.

At night, the gentle floodlighting of the fortress accentuates the charm of old stone. The church clock, which repeats its strike on the hour, adds to the atmosphere. One sleeps safely within the ramparts.

POUSADA ACTIVITIES

Family games and snooker.

AREA ACTIVITIES

Shooting, fishing (river), golf, country walks, cycling, cruises, four-wheel driving, four-wheel motorbikes, sailing, rowing, canoeing, swimming pool, horse-riding and carriage tours.

HOW TO FIND

Easy. Inside the old fortifications of Vila Nova de Cerveira. Like Valença (13kms south-west), Vila Nova de Cerveira stands on the River Minho, 39 kms from Viana do Castelo.

São Teotónio is in a different category to its neighbour, Dom Dinis at Vila Nova de Cerveira (regional rather than historical), and it is no bad thing to have these two pousadas competing for business. It ensures a healthy rivalry and high standards. The pousada, which is named after Portugal's first saint, was purpose-built in 1962. It is well-established and popular, with lovely river views from the reception rooms and spacious bedrooms.

The fortress town of Valença is a great tourist attraction and, despite the inevitable souvenir shops geared to this passing trade, the town has retained its charm with its narrow cobbled streets, squares and fountains. It is reminiscent of Óbidos, north of Lisbon, where there is another pousada. Both towns, fortunately, are scheduled as national monuments.

The origin of the Valença is uncertain, but from Roman times it was known as Contrasta. At the beginning of the

> *named after Portugal's first saint ... well-established and popular, with lovely river views* "

POUSADA DE VALENÇA DO MINHO

São Teotónio

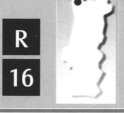

R

16

POUSADA ACTIVITIES

family games.

AREA ACTIVITIES

river fishing, rowing, canoeing, country walks, beaches, swimming pool and golf.

HOW TO FIND

Easy. Inside the old fortress in Valença, on the north-east corner overlooking the bridge across the river into Spain. Valença is in the far north of Portugal on the road on the Portuguese side of the River Minho.

13th century, King Sancho I erected a castle here. King Afonso III (1248-1279) changed the name to Valença, but quite why is not clear. Several succeeding kings continued defensive works and by the beginning of the 18th century the town had become one of the most important and largest fortresses in Portugal. The emblazoned gateways were guarded by cannons which are still in place around the ramparts. Despite several sieges, some by the French, the original fortifications are in a very good state of preservation.

There are an increasing number of river crossings into Spain both by ferry and bridges, but on the Portuguese side Ponte de Lima, Ponte da Barca and Monção are riverside towns of charm and interest. This is the area of country houses and the distinctive granaries built on stone stilts to protect the corn from predators.

Of all the country houses there is nothing to rival Brejoeira Palace, 5 kms south of Monção. Although access even to the grounds is not permitted, it is nice to stand and stare. Built in the first half of the 19th century on much the same lines as the Ajuda Palace in Lisbon, it was sold at public auction in 1901 and now produces the very up-market and expensive 'Alvarinho' *vinho verde.* You will notice on your travels the vines growing on supported pergolas. These grow the grapes from which the *vinho verde* is produced.

Looking across the Minho as the lights come on in Spain, you are conscious of the closeness of another country with its own separate culture and customs. On whichever side of the border you come to rest for the night, it would be difficult to beat the Pousada de São Teotónio.

S ituated within 10 kms of the small agricultural town of Amares, itself about 20 kms northeast of Braga, this 12th-century ruined Benedictine or Cistercian monastery has been saved from further deterioration by ENATUR. It has been converted into a pousada as have so many other ancient Portuguese monuments.

Categorised an historical pousada, the architects had a delightful building to work on. Much altered and enlarged in the 18th century, the place had been

ransacked over the years and much iron, lead and statuary stolen or vandalized. As with São Francisco in Beja, which was in a similar sad state, Santa Maria do Bouro opened with much of its former wall paintings and *azulejos* restored. Some of them date back to the 17th century and depict the life of St Bernard.

With the pousada at Viana do Castelo and the one at Caniçada, this most attractive corner of the Minho is well served with accommodation.

Abadia is an 18th-century sanctuary, near the pousada, from which there is a fine view.

The two rivers of Cavado and Homem add greatly to the charm of the region, is a prolific orange-growing area. There are a number of stylish country houses and remains of earlier man's occupation of these parts, as well as the nearby spa of Caldelas.

Top left: Haystacks, Minho-style.
Top right: Bom Jesus do Monte stairway.
Centre, left & right: The Pousada.

**POUSADA
DE AMARES**

> " *a 12th century monastery,
> saved and converted into a pousada
> with much of its former wall paintings
> and azulejos restored* "

Santa Maria
do Bouro

**H
32**

POUSADA ACTIVITIES

*Swimming pool, tennis,
snooker, walks in the
countryside and family
games.*

AREA ACTIVITIES

*Fishing (river), horse
riding, bicycle tours,
four-wheel driving,
cruises, Gerês mountain
range tracks, bird
watching, golf, water
sports, shooting range and
paintball.*

HOW TO FIND

*Easy. After Amares,
take the Gerês road
to the village of Bouro
Santa Maria (10 kms).
The pousada is in the
centre of this village,
on the right side of
the road.*

An away-from-it-all feeling greets you on driving into the courtyard. This lovely hostelry is, aesthetically, one of the most successful of the modern pousadas. Unlike many pousadas overlooking dams (*barragens*), it is not an adaptation of buildings used in the dam's construction (1952-4). Originally a hunting lodge, it was acquired and opened as a pousada in 1968 and has an established reputation for food and comfort. The central heating and galleried

sala (sitting-room) make for a cosy sojourn in winter. The high ceilings are in wood, supported on joists with massive rafters and purlins, all adding to the hunting lodge atmosphere. The large shaded picture windows overlooking the lake and mountains make it pleasantly cool in summer.

Gerês, the nearest town, is a popular spa. King Luis I took the cure there in 1888. It was not as efficacious as he hoped - he died the following year! In the pump room and the rather faded hotels there is a hint of past glories. The whole area forms part of the Peneda-Gerês National Park of

we are now amongst the best scenery Portugal, if not Europe, has to offer

R

29

about 70,000 hectares (175.000 sq. miles). This is a mature reserve where bird-watchers have every chance of seeing a wide range of species including eagles. Also on the park are wild ponies and pigs, deer, wolves and genets. The tourist office by the pump room and the national park office can give the answer to most questions.

There are suggested walks to suit the individual. For a debut, try Pedra Bela (6.5 kms). If you want a sterner test, have a go at Bouça da Mó (20 kms). The tourist office will tell you the nearest point a taxi can reach. The park is equally rewarding for the nature lover who just likes strolling amid the scents and sounds of streams and forest. If you want to shoot or fish, details can be obtained from the pousada or the tourist office. In the main, the park is concerned with conservation, so these sports are very strictly controlled, but there are other possibilities outside. In the park there are so many different trees that an identification book is useful. There is plenty of heather sweeping up towards a dusting of winter snow on the peaks which rise to 1,500 metres.

We are now amongst the best scenery Portugal, if not Europe, has to offer. Standing on the upper slopes of the Serra do Gerês or on the Serra do Barroso, the river Cavado way below looks minute. Even the great lakes along its course look like puddles, and the houses around the shore appear merely as specks. There are a million and one places from which to enjoy the scenery, but probably none better than from the terrace of the pousada.

POUSADA ACTIVITIES

Swimming pool, tennis court and family games

AREA ACTIVITIES

Shooting, fishing (dam), water sports (dam), cruises, horse riding, country walks, natural park walks and gymnasium (spa).

HOW TO FIND

Take the main road east from Braga to Chaves. After about 30kms, there is a road on the left to Caniçada village and Caldas do Gerês. After about 1km, the pousada is on your right.

W hen Santa Marinha opened in 1985 it was, without doubt, one of the fabulous jewels in the crown of Portugal's pousadas. Since then a number of new pousadas in the south can claim to rival its opulence. Nevertheless, it is a palatial and impressive building and one of the outstanding hotels in the Iberian peninsula.

To use the word 'palatial' is not an exaggeration. It takes time to absorb its vastness. Just when you think the layout has been mastered - from the reception area through the tiled and sunken bar and lounge to the vaulted dining-room - you discover that much remains. There are discreet cloisters and there is the São Jerónimo fountain at the end of the fantastically long bedrooms corridor where, it is rumoured, Sr Leite de Castro, the last private owner, exercised his horse. The anteroom is decorated with 16th-century *azulejos* by Policarpo Oliveira Bernardes. As if the foregoing was not enough, the enormous and sumptuously furnished drawing-room of about 240 square metres awaits you. There are

POUSADA DE GUIMARÃES

Santa
Marinha

H
51

POUSADA ACTIVITIES

Family games.

AREA ACTIVITIES

Horse riding, shooting range, country walks, four-wheel driving, traditional games, paintball, mountain bikes excursions, micro lighting and golf.

HOW TO FIND

Needs care. From Guimarães take the N 101 to Penha (east of Guimarães). After 2kms, at Costa, take a small road to the left leading to the pousada, which is next door to the church.

51 bedrooms, two suites, lift, air-conditioning and central heating. The whole is set in wooded grounds of 12 hectares (30 acres).

The earliest written evidence concerning the site was in 959 AD when, in the will of Mumadona, the property 'Lourosa' was left to the Monastery of Guimarães. There is a Praça de Mumadona adjoining the Ducal Palace of Bragança at the junction of Rua Serpa Pinto and Rua D. Constança de Noronha. There is little doubt that Lourosa included Santa Marinha da Costa and that Queen Mafalda, wife of King Afonso Henriques, established a religious order for the canons of St Augustine. In 1528 the Duke of Bragança obtained the Pope's authorisation to establish a monastery for the monks of São Jerónimo and it seems probable António Crato received his education here. He was the last of the Grand Priors of a branch of the Knights Hospitallers. Before dying in Paris in 1595 he made a couple of attempts to claim the Portuguese throne.*(See Pousada Flor da Rosa, Crato)*

In 1834 many lands belonging to the church were secularised and Santa Marinha da Costa passed to Dom António de Araujo Fernandes Leite de Castro. At the same time it was designated as a building of national importance, which it remains today. Later the Jesuits occupied the monastery until the buildings were devasted by a major fire in 1951. Thereafter, the Leite de Castro family lived in the rambling and deteriorating mansion until it was acquired for conversion into a pousada in 1975.

When the pousada first opened, there was a museum-like atmosphere in which flowers, ticking clocks

and the sound of laughter were missing. The crown of Santa Marinha sat precariously and self-consciously on her head. Now, it is a very different place. Time and good management have produced a reputation for good food and service. Tradition is not created overnight.

Apart from sightseeing in the town centre of Guimarães, where there is another pousada, the neighbouring towns of Braga (22 kms) and Barcelos (4 kms) warrant a visit. Braga is sometimes called 'Portugal's Rome', presumably because of the large number of fountains and churches and the fact that the Roman Catholic Primate of Portugal is the Archbishop of Braga. It has some fine domestic architecture and like most historic towns it is best explored on foot. As good a place as any to start is the tourist office in Praça da República where useful advice can be obtained.

Have a look at the 16th-century Casa dos Cravos, the Archbishop's Palace, the Cathedral, the 14th-century King's Chapel and the 17th-century mansion called Casa dos Biscainhos. The local councillors have done themselves well in the Praça do Município, and another fine building is the ornate Casa do Mexicano (or Palácio do Raio).

On the outskirts, Bom Jesus is a much visited church. Whether the steps are worth climbing is a matter of personal choice. Even from the bottom it is impressive.

Barcelos is another ancient town. The outskirts, with hideous developments like the high-rise Santa Clara complex and the scattering of industrial buildings in all directions, are inclined to put off most people. Persevere if only to track down the Cock of Barcelos which is almost as famous as the national emblem of France.

The general theme of the legend is that a criminal in the 14th century was sentenced to death. He vehemently proclaimed his innocence and told the judge that to prove it, a cock would crow. That night at dinner the judge was about to carve his chicken when the bird let forth a 'cock-a-doodle-do' of such sincerity and intensity, he ordered the prisoner's release. In the former ducal palace there is some statuary erected, it is claimed, by the released prisoner. A pinch of salt with your chicken might be the order of the day, but the legend has provided the excuse to produce millions of gaudy cockerels. The tourist office in the Torre de Menagem has more cockerels in every conceivable size than it has literature.

The pousada buildings date back to the 13th century. Originally private houses, much modified over the generations, they were acquired by ENATUR and opened as a pousada in 1980. It is a lovely old hostelry in the centre of the town, with all the friendly personal atmosphere of a family-run coaching house. Beamed ceilings, studded leather chairs, antique paintings and gentle lighting extend a warmth of welcome which comes with the years. It is lived in and loved, alive and unpretentious but lacking nothing in comfort or cuisine. Fortunately in this congested town centre, several parking lots are reserved for guests.

Guimarães was the original capital of Portugal and birthplace of D. Afonso Henriques (1139-85), the country's first king. Is a lovely old town steeped in history and rightly called the cradle of Portugal. Its plethora of churches, chapels, convents and museums make it happy fodder for the guide books, but the stamp of Guimarães is indelibly printed in the memory by the minor houses emblazoned with coats of arms, by the arcaded streets with pillars rubbed smooth by centuries of passers-by, and by the narrow alleyways with verandas leaning forward to greet their opposite neighbours.

At the foot of the 10th-century castle where Afonso Henriques was born, is the massive Ducal Palace, erected by the first Duke of Bragança in the 15th century. The Braganças ruled Portugal from 1640 until the fall of the monarchy in 1910. Most people find the interior furniture and furnishings rather more agreeable than the somewhat forbidding and uncompromising lines of the exterior.

In the Largo da Oliveira, the pousada is ideally situated for exploring the many

POUSADA DE
GUIMARÃES

Nossa Senhora
da Oliveira

R
16

POUSADA ACTIVITIES

Family games.

AREA ACTIVITIES

*Golf, swimming pool, horse
riding and shooting range.*

HOW TO FIND

*Very easy. In the
centre of the historic
city of Guimarães
which lies 22km
south-west
of Braga and
49km north-east
of Oporto.*

attractions of the town's centre. A street map is useful.
One can be obtained in the tourist office in Alameda da
Liberdade gardens, south of the pousada. Close by, the
São Francisco and the Santos Passos churches can be
inspected. The local councillors have installed themselves in what was the Convento de Santa Clara, a fine
building with a baroque facade built in 1741. At the
rear, have a glimpse at the Praça de Santiago. In the
Largo da Oliveira is the crenellated Paços do Concelho
commenced during King João's reign (1385-1433). At
street level, massive pillars give welcome shade in hot
weather. In the square, the church of Nossa Senhora da
Oliveira was founded by Countess Mumadona in the
10th century. It was largely rebuilt by João I after his
victorious battle at Aljubarrota and much modernised
over the centuries. (*See Pousada Mestre Afonso
Domingues, Batalha*)

Adjoining the cloisters is the Alberto Sampaio Museum and not far distant the Martins Sarmento, which
will interest archaeologists. The area adjoining Largo
do Toural has several period houses, some of the ground
floors having been converted into shops.

The pousada gets its name from the legend of King
Wamba, a Visigoth who lived somewhere around the
mid-7th century. He did not care for the idea of ruling
and said he would only do so if the olive branch staff he
was carrying sprouted when he thrust it into the ground.
It did and he became king!

Above: The Pousada in the Largo da Oliveira

The Province of Trás-os-Montes

> *a little-explored land of myths and legends*

This remote and romantic province in the extreme northeast corner of the country is a land of myths and legends, little explored by the foreign visitor until major east/west trunk roads brought the fascinating towns of Vila Real, Chaves and Bragança within easy reach of the traveller.

There are still parts of Trás-os-Montes, in the Serras of Montezinho, Coro, Nogueira and Marão for example, where village life has changed little over the centuries. It is surprising, therefore, to find locals approaching you in remotest villages with a pretty good knowledge of English or French or German. The reason is that extreme poverty in these poorer agricultural areas has meant that young people have left to seek their fortunes in more prosperous European countries, even working as far afield as Canada and America. The pull of the homeland is very strong in the Portuguese character and many return with their hard-saved 'nest-egg'. Very often, with the aid of similarly placed friends, they build their retirement homes, sometimes with more enthusiasm than taste. If you come across a remote pseudo Swiss-type chalet, you may be pretty sure of its background.

Early man roamed these wilds and there are many monuments to his occupation. The giant granite boar at Murça on the southern slopes of the Serra do Vilrelho,

Opposite top: The village of Mazouco
Opposite centre and bellow: Bragança Castle at dawn and sunset
Top and centre right: In festive mood
Below right: Harvesting the grapes

quite near the pousada at Alijó, is a good example of pre-Christian occupation
There are many others. Porca de Murça, as it is known, gives its name to a good and
inexpensive wine. The fertile valleys where the climate is gentler than on the higher
ground, the forests, and the ample water which has enabled the great spas of Vidago
and Chaves to flourish, all played their part in encouraging our predecessors to settle
here. Wild animals still hit the headlines of national newspapers when a wolf attacks
cattle or a villager is gored by a wild boar.

Trás-os-Montes includes the more civilised Alto Douro. Some of the wine *quintas*
overlooking the Douro are the homes of wealthy port producers, for it is here, around
Peso de Régua and Pinhão, that the best grapes are grown. The local reds, not unlike
a very young Beaujolais, are light, refreshing and go down well with a chunk of new
bread and a thin slice of Chaves smoked ham (*presunto*).

Only the mysticism and time-warp atmosphere of Trás-os-Montes could produce

the unique *vinho dos mortos* (wine of the dead). Buried by the locals of Boticas during the Napoleonic wars to avoid confiscation by the French invaders (sometimes in the cemetery where freshly turned earth was less conspicuous), it was found to be better in colour and taste when it was retrieved some years later.

Outside Vila Real you will recognise the Count of Vila Real's Solar Mateus: a picture of its facade graces each bottle of the ubiquitous Mateus Rosé. Near the Alijó pousada at Carrazeda de Ansiães, there is reputed to be the great granite boulder in Bulideira which, despite its gigantic size, a child can rock. I use the word 'reputed' because I have not seen it and the guide books are divergent in their views as to its location. It may be one of the many Trás-os Montes legends. I am determined to find it and give it a shove!

Opposite page : The meandering Douro. Top: Port wine country. Bellow:Transporting barrels downriver.

T his pousada celebrated its 25th anniversary in 1984 and the special velvet-bound and embroidered guest book for that year shows how wide is its appeal. Signatures of professors from Switzerland, doctors from St. Bartholomew's Hospital in London and visitors from New York, Germany, Denmark and elsewhere make interesting reading.

The pousada is well located, looking across a valley at the floodlit castle. The town may be approached by the IP4 from Vila Real (138 kms) or the more northerly EN103, via Chaves (65 kms). If you can make a circular tour, you will enjoy spectacular mountain scenery. On the southern route, Romeu, a small village on the south of the road before Mirandela, has a small museum. 11,000 square metres of roof were renewed to restore this dying village, thanks mainly to a local port wine king, José Menéres. The IP2 is a good approach from Guarda in the south.

Bragança is the most northeasterly town in Portugal, over 500 kms from Lisbon and only 30 kms from Spain. To the north, the Serra de Montezinho national park can be explored on foot or by car. From it, on a clear day, the sun shines on the distant snow-capped peaks of Spain's Sierra de la Cabrera (2,200 metres). To the south, the town is protected by the Serra da Nogueira. There is a feeling of remoteness in these parts. It is a land of mystery and myth where, in the past, minorities have taken up residence in order to avoid persecution. Jewish refugees from the Inquisition came to settle and as recently as 1927 their descendents opened a synagogue.

Improved motor links have made access easier, but have not dispelled the haunting atmosphere of this isolated and neglected backwater. Many of the care-

fully preserved rites and festivals are more pagan than Christian. The masks worn by the children - and the not-so-young - between Christmas and 6th January (Day of the Kings in Portugal) are pretty horrendous.

There is much to interest the visitor. Take the N103 to ancient Vinhais, not forgetting to inspec en route the strange and disintegrating monas tery of Castro de Avelas (5 kms). In Vinhais there are several houses of note and the 17th-centur fountain in the Largo do Arrabalde, bearing th

> *the pousada is well located, looking across the valley at the floodlit castle, the original seat of the Bragança's*

São
Bartolomeu

R

28

coat of arms of the Count of Arrabalde, is charming. On the other side of the town, the N308 and N218 lead to Gimonde with its Roman bridge, and Outeiro whose Santo Cristo church and Gothic pillory make a rewarding excursion. Izeda (40 kms) on the N217 is another fascinating old town.

From the pousada terrace there is a view of the castle, the original seat of the ruling Braganças. Probably the most interesting building is the medieval Domus Municipais, a town hall on Roman foundations. If it is not open, ask at the tourist office for the key. The Princess Tower of the castle and the old cathedral both have early pillories nearby. Also within the ramparts is the church of Santa Maria. The Museum of Abade de Baçal is located in the former Bishop's Palace. The church of São Vincente is reputedly where King Pedro married his lover. (For the story of King Pedro and Inês de Castro, see the chapter on Mestre Afonso Domingues pousada at Batalha).

It is always an experience to sip a drink on the terrace and look across at the Braganças. History looks back at you.

POUSADA ACTIVITIES

Swimming pool and family games.

AREA ACTIVITIES

Shooting, fishing, four-wheel driving, micro lighting, shooting range.

HOW TO FIND

Straightforward. On the outskirts of Bragança (in Portugal's most north-easterly corner) coming from Vila Real (south-west). The pousada is in the Estrada do Turismo, on the right.

Perched on the edge of the rocky gorge of the Barragem of Miranda do Douro, this pousada was originally built in connection with a joint Portuguese and Spanish project to establish a chain of dams along the Douro to provide hydro-electric power. It was subsequently adapted and opened as a pousada in 1962. A road now runs across the dam, the centre of which is the boundary between the two countries. It can be seen from the terrace, public rooms and bedrooms. It is an unforgettable view. The agitated flow of this long, natural river running from deep inside Spain right across Portugal to Oporto has been tamed and harnessed by the skill of engineers to form a peaceful lake. Vultures wheel in the sky. Gulls appear like confetti on the waters below. With luck you may see a golden eagle. Bird identification books at the

> *from the terrace there is the feeling you could almost touch Spain on the other side of this sheer, rock-faced gorge*

POUSADA DE MIRANDA DO DOURO

Santa Catarina

R

12

POUSADA ACTIVITIES

Family games

AREA ACTIVITIES

Shooting (partridge, rabbit and wild boar), fishing (river), cruises, country walks, cycling, canoeing, swimming pool.

ready, it is a great place for ornithologists.

From the terrace there is the feeling you could almost touch Spain on the other side of this sheer, rock-faced gorge. It is interesting to try to pick out which is Portugal and which is Spain as the river interlaces the ravines. Like a maze, it is more difficult than you would think.

The sense of being able to reach across to make contact with Spain was acknowledged by Wellington. When wishing to visit his troops in Portugal, he decided the quickest way was to be winched across the ravine. The year was 1813. The great soldier had already proved himself a man of exceptional military perspicacity. He must also have possessed an exceptional head for heights!

Public rooms and bedrooms are spacious and there is a very good terrace from which to enjoy this impressive and unique outlook.

HOW TO FIND
Easy. In the centre of Miranda do Douro. In the Estrada da Barragem (the road to the lake), on the left, next to the branch of the Banco Português do Atlântico (BPA).

Because of its remoteness, several customs have survived longer than in more accessible parts. A tongue derived from Latin, known as Mirandês, is still heard in the villages. There are many local customs and legends whose origins are lost in the mists of time. One concerns Miranda do Douro's 16th-century cathedral in which little Jesus is the proud possessor of a top hat! Legend has it that a young lad enthusiastically urged his seniors to resist the Spanish invaders. Spurred on by his shouts of encouragement, they were successful. Despite the fact that the young man disappeared after the battle, the town wished to honour the event. A statuette was made of young Jesus surmounted, not by a crown of thorns, but a top hat.

Another custom centred around the cathedral occurs on Christmas Day. It is called *Fogueira do galo* meaning Christmas bonfire. (*Missa do galo* is Christmas midnight mass). The young bachelors of the town are directed by an annually elected council of six senior citizens to collect a mountain of firewood in carts and deposit it in the churchyard. In front of the ensuing blaze the folk of Miranda do Douro gather (it can be bitterly cold at this time of the year). Failure to discharge their task conscientiously results in a fine, payable in wine. There is much merriment and the bachelor of this year may well meet his bride of next year. Nobody knows how long this tradition has been in existence. Yet another custom surviving the centuries is the *pauliteiros* dance performed on the third Sunday of August. A *pauliteiros* is a kind of sword fight with sticks, accompanied by the rhythm of tambourines and bagpipes. Do not confuse it with *paliteiro* - a toothpick holder!

People from these parts are proud and independent. They have a rhyming legend '*P'ra cá do Marão mandam os que cá estão, e p'ra lá mandarão ou não*'. Roughly

translated it means: 'We on this side of the mountains of Marão (the province's southern boundary) are rulers - on the other side not necessarily so'. Remember, the House of Bragança from Trás-os-Montes ruled Portugal from 1640 to the end of the monarchy in 1910.

The countryside between Miranda do Douro and Bragança is often reminiscent of parts of Britain. There is little traffic on the secondary roads, which adds to the sense of remoteness. Along the roadside are cherry trees and wild dog roses. Agriculture is more productive than it used to be because of modern machinery purchased by itinerant Portuguese workers. The pockets of vines increase as Miranda is approached. There are a few large fields of corn, but in the main it is the ever changing character that impresses; here an orchard, there a clump of pines and a

Opposite top: Child Jesus in top hat.
Previous pages and opposite bellow: The pousada.
Above: Miranda do Douro dam.
Left: Trás-os-Montes pigeon loft.

few small fields of vegetables, particularly on the outskirts of rare and scattered villages. White marble and wolfram are local products.

The inverted horse's hoof-like buildings may puzzle you. They are dotted about in no particular fashion. They are pigeon-lofts, although little used today. In past days when a holding was divided between inheriting children, the one who came by the pigeon-loft was often better off than those inheriting the house!

Santa Catarina hasn't the casual passing trade of the more centrally located pousadas. By and large travellers don't happen to be in Miranda do Douro by chance; they have made a special journey. There is always a warm welcome from people of these parts and from the staff and director of Santa Catarina.

It would be difficult to stay at Barão de Forrester without acquiring a knowledge, however eclectic, of the production of port wine. All around are *quintas*, owners and workers involved with its production. Barão Forrester (the *de* seems optional) is part of the history of port wine. As a young man, James Forrester (1809-1862) came to work in his uncle's firm, Offley Forrester and Co. By all

accounts he was a gifted man who, unlike some of his compatriots, mastered the language and integrated into Portuguese society. He was an artist and a cartographer. A copy of his map of the Douro hangs in the pousada. He was a purist in his desire to keep port as a pure wine, unfortified by brandy and coloured by elderberries. He eventually lost the battle with brandy, but scored a success against elderberries. The pousada has a model of the *rabelo* from which, on 12th May 1862, Forrester fell and was drowned, though not before he had been created a Baron by the King of Portugal, an honour also bestowed on an earlier merchant, John Croft, who was given the title Barão de Estrela.

The *rabelo*, so called because of its long tail-like steering oar, was the original method of transporting the wine from the *quintas* downstream to the warehouses at Vila Nova de Gaia, opposite Oporto. If you take the steep N322 to Pinhão and, after

> ❝*Barão de Forrester is part of the history of port wine*❞

R

21

rossing the bridge, follow the Douro to Régua, you will see some famous names on the steeply terraced ills. Names like Sandeman, Noval, Fonseca, Offley, Carvalhas of the Real Companhia Velha, Croft's Quinta le Roeda and, upstream, Quinta de Vesúvia owned by Ferreira, Warre's Quinta do Bonfim, Quinta do nfantado and many more.

The *rabelo* gave way to the train which in turn was uperseded by the motorised tanker which speedily ransport the wine to Vila Nova de Gaia. Traditions die ard, particularly in the port wine business, but moored utside the warehouse you may still see the old faithfuls f the lovely river Douro. Also, several of the major roducers stage an illustrated lecture over a glass of heir wine.

Lamego is only 15 kms south of Régua and if a redilection for port can be overcome, a visit is rewarding. The Sanctuary of our Lady of Redemption, vith its 286 steps, is very much like the Bom Jesus at Braga and gives a fine view of the town. Lamego is enowned for its pottery and there are good examples f decorative tiles on several buildings.

POUSADA ACTIVITIES

Swimming pool, tennis and family games.

AREA ACTIVITIES

Shooting, fishing, water sports, country walks, bicycle tours, gymnasium, shooting range and 'quintas' tours.

HOW TO FIND

Easy. In the town of Alijó, next door to the Post Office (Correio). To get to Alijó take the road from Vila Real to Bragança. Some kilometres before Murça, a road to the right leads south to Alijó.

lthough a very small province in the north with an area of only 3,334 sq kms, Douro Litoral has some marvellous scenery, an interesting coastline and is the home of Portugal's second largest city - Oporto (Porto in Portuguese). It is from this area, known in Roman times as Portucale, that the country gets its name, but to most of us the association is with the wine of the region, the ever popular port wine. Strangely, port is more popular out of the country than in it.

Oporto cascades clumsily down the northern banks of the river Douro and faces Vila Nova de Gaia where the great warehouses storing the port wine are located. The waterfront has a disorganised charm not dissimilar to the Alfama district of Lisbon. There are many little restaurants serving pretty good and inexpensive food. You may not like tripe, but it is the staple diet of the residents of Oporto, so much so that they are often referred to as *Tripeiros*. Give it a try as you sit overlooking the river of gold, for this is what Douro means. A number of bridges span the river. Pleasure boats ply up and down taking visitors on short or long trips.

Oporto is an industrial town, but it has some attractive buildings and parks. Perhaps the most surprising building is the Stock Exchange. Put up to impress, its pseudo Moorish style certainly impresses, but whether with good taste or not is another matter. The port wine trade was very much a British prerogative and British influence still forms part of Oporto's society. It is not only for port that the area is known: *vinho verde* (green wine) is also popular, although the best, 'Alvarinho,' comes from further north.

The busy and attractive fishing towns of Vila do Conde and Póvoa do Varzim north of the Douro are popular tourist areas, but the fashionable resort for the *Tripeiros* is Espinho, 15 kms south of the city.

There are two pousadas in the Douro Litoral, good bases from which to explore the

The Province of Douro Litoral

"marvellous scenery, an interesting coastline and the home of Portugal's second largest city"

Opposite Top: The home of Mateus Rosé
Opposite below: Amarante
Left: Oporto riverfront
Above: Grape harvesting
Below: Chapel near Amarante

province. São Gonçalo is near the town of Amarante; Solar da Rede, to the southeast, is near Mesão Frio on the river Douro. Much of the Douro is dammed to provide hydroelectric power and irrigation. The resulting great artificial lakes of Carrapatelo and Torrão have enhanced rather than detracted from the natural beauty of the region.

There are any number of local crafts still prospering: weaving, embroidery, the making of models in wood, clay and metal, and even the manufacture of straw hats.

The province is not as well-known to foreigners as it should be.

A lthough the new east-west IP4 has greatly increased the accessibility of these afforested mountains, the pousada still retains the welcoming atmosphere of an isolated retreat and is a good central location from which to explore the area and the towns on either side - Amarante and Vila Real (20 kms). It is a warm comfortable hostelry in winter and a cool mountain retreat in the summer.

There are some good local wines from the neighbouring towns and the staff were helpful with their suggestions. Without doubt the best promoted and internationally known local wine is Mateus Rosé. Each flagon-type bottle bears a picture of the Count of Vila Real's country home to the east of the town. It is open to the public. Perhaps a trifle too baroque for the purist, the lakeside setting reduces the excesses and produces a distinctive and acceptable whole. The characteristic style of the 18th-century architect Nicolau Nasoni can also be evidenced in his Capela Nova in the town.

Although Vila Real has an attractive setting, amid the verdant valleys of the Corgo and Cabril where vines and fruit flourish and there are some good 16th- and

POUSADA ACTIVITIES

Mountain biking and family games.

AREA ACTIVITIES

Countryside walking excursions, golf and shooting.

HOW TO FIND

Easy. Off the main road IP4 from Oporto to Vila Real, about midway between Amarante (24kms) and Vila Real (20kms).

> *although increasingly accessible, the pousada retains the welcoming atmosphere of an isolated retreat*

17th-century houses, it is Amarante which is the more attractive. This may be due to its romantic associations.

Amarante is an ancient town which has developed at the crossing of the river Tâmega. Dominating the town and looking down regally on the river is the convent and church of São Gonçalo (from which the pousada gets its name). It is a pleasing and imposing 16th-century building in which Gonçalo, the local saint, is buried. The tomb must have been moved there, as the convent had not been founded in the 13th century when he died. Gonçalo is the patron saint of lovers and it is claimed that husband seekers may be certain of marrying within the year if they rub their naked flesh against his tomb. To increase the chances of matrimony, a *Bolinho de amor* might just do the trick. This is a sponge-cake baked in phallic form and offered during the first week of June, a custom probably dating back to a pre-Christian fertility cult. The *Blue Guide to Portugal*, referring to the bridge, tells us that Gonçalo's erection collapsed in 1763. It seems doubtful, therefore, whether the spell of tomb and sponge-cake will be as efficacious as was planned!

Another erogenous-sounding cake is *Papo de Anjo* (angel's breast), well-known as a local sweet but rather less exciting than it sounds. Felgueiras, on the N101 Guimarães road, makes a less erotic cake by the name of *Margarida* and also produces some fine lacework.

We have always enjoyed our stays at São Gonçalo. There is plenty of interest in the villages and surrounding countryside and a comfortable welcome after a day out.

in 27 hectares of vineyard, with a commanding position overlooking the Douro river

The opening of this pousada at the end of 1998 provided much needed accommodation. The only other hotel of quality in the region is upstream at Pinhão where Taylors have recently opened the Vintage House Hotel.

Solar da Rede is a converted 18th century manor house (*solar* is Portuguese for manor house). It stands in 27 hectares of vineyard and has a commanding position overlooking the Douro river. It is off the road between Mesão Frio and Régua at the village of Santa Cristina. Although in a relatively isolated part of Portugal, there is much to do and see. The pousada offers tennis and a good swimming pool, but the river is the focal point where fishing, boating and river cruises can all be enjoyed. Even a train journey following the banks of the Douro is well worthwhile and, if you can make time, the *azulejos* panels on the station at Pinhão depict life in this heart of the port wine countryside. If my addition is correct there are 24 and just by studying them it is easy to imagine the life of those concerned with the production of the famous drink. The straw capes worn when pruning the vines in the bitter winter weather could become a *haute couture* fashion. Certainly they would be considerably more practical than much that is disported on the catwalks of London and Paris.

This is an area where primitive man settled and traces of early civilisations are abundant. In Mesão Frio the church of St. Nicholas (*Nicolau*) is a masterpiece of

POUSADA DE MESÃO FRIO

Solar da Rede

H

31

POUSADA ACTIVITIES

Family games, swimming pool, tennis, countryside activities, snooker, bird-watching.

AREA ACTIVITIES

Shooting, fishing, golf, river cruising, countryside bicycle excursions, nature trails.

HOW TO FIND

Easy. At the village of Santa Cristina just off the EN 100 between Régua (8 km) and Mesão Frio (1 km).

baroque architecture. Originally Gothic, it was substantially altered in the 18th century with some good carvings and masses of gilt. You are near enough to include visits to Lamego, Amarante and the manor house to beat all manor houses, Mateus, on the outskirts of Vila Real.

The pousada is very comfortable. The bedrooms on the first floor are approached by the original staircase. The high standard of food is typical of the Douro and Trás-os-Montes.

The wines of the Douro need some beating. Although very much overshadowed by the widely advertised and marketed Port, the red table wines from this region can hold their own in any company. This is also an area of the *vinho verde* which, although a little acidic for many, can provide a refreshing drink on a hot summer's day. Experiment with white Port and a splash of tonic - a worthy rival to the ubiquitous "gin and tonic".

It would be sacrilege whilst in Douro not to have a glass of Port and here one is spoilt for choice. If you want to know more about Port, a visit downstream to Vila Nova de Gaia and one of the warehouses of a major producer will greatly increase your knowledge. Also, read the chapter on the pousada Barão de Forrester at Alijó.

The area is essentially an agricultural one with wine production the predominant occupation. Nevertheless, if you need a new straw hat you can have one made to measure at Tendais (south of Cinfães). Local crafts are still alive and flourishing in this most attractive and magnetic corner of Portugal. You will return to Solar da Rede.

The Province of Beira

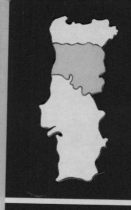

" a great band of land running across Portugal from the Atlantic to the Spanish border "

Beira, with an area of 27,398 sq kms, is fractionally bigger than the Alentejo and is Portugal's largest province. It is bounded by the river Douro in the north and the Tagus in the south. It is a great band of land running across Portugal from the Atlantic in the west to the Spanish border in the east. Because of its size, it is divided administratively into three: Beira Alta (upper), Beira Baixa (lower) and Beira Litoral (coastal). Despite its size, it currently possesses only half as many pousadas as the Alentejo. It is a province of considerable scenic variation and it may be convenient to deal with these variations under the three sections mentioned.

Beira Litoral

Until the middle of the last century it was known as Beira-Mar (beside the sea) and occupies a strip of land running from Ovar in the north to the spa town of Monte Real in the south. It is at its widest around the latitude of the major town of Coimbra - a marvellous old university town steeped in history and learning. Flatter than the other subdivisions, Beira Litoral includes Aveiro, the 'Venice of Portugal', which can be explored from the coastal pousada at Ria. The other pousadas in the Litoral are Santa Cristina at Condeixa-a-Nova 15 kms north of Coimbra, Mestre Domingues adjoining the breathtaking Batalha (Battle) Abbey, and the most recently opened, Conde de Ourém.

Top: Aveiro waterfront.
Centre: A quiet corner in Oliveira do Hospital
Below: Fátima Shrine

The Litoral is interlaced with attractive rivers like the Vouga and Mondego. Coarse fishing is a popular pastime. In the smaller tributaries, such as Alfusqueiro, Antuão and Caima, there are trout if you prefer fly-ishing. Coupled with the various types of shellfish from the Atlantic shores, there is always a good choice of

fish on most menus. The mouth of the major rivers makes an ideal location for salt flats, which are still developed commercially.

The best-known and most popular of the seaside resorts is Figueira da Foz, a sizeable town with all the fun of the fair at hand. You may prefer the smaller and more secluded beaches of Mira or Tocha. All have superb sands.

Travelling east, the dunes, salt flats and river estuaries give way to cultivated farm land, vineyards producing the highly-rated Bairrada vintages, and thence to the great sweeps of the mountain ranges of Buçaco, Lousa and Caramulo. It is lovely countryside. In the remote villages and in the towns of Leiria and Pombal, and the great spas of Curia and Luso, the traveller senses he has set foot in the 'real' Portugal and feels enriched by so doing.

Beira Alta

In the past, Beira Alta was often called 'Beira Transmontana'. It is with the great snowcapped ranges of the Serra da Estrela (2,000 metres) and its foothills that this region is associated. It is a wild and rugged landscape softening as the mountain

slopes descend to the fertile river valleys of the Mondego and Dão, where the regional wine is becoming as well-known outside Portugal as it is in. The two towns of the area are Guarda and Viseu. Both are sizeable and can provide the visitor with hours of pleasure, given the time to explore them.

Guarda, the highest town in Portugal, has a long history of repelling invaders. A giant cathedral dominates the town, and the nearby reorganised museum gives a display of artefacts from past centuries. Viseu is also dominated by its cathedral and like Guarda has used the Bishop's Palace as a museum. The Grão Vasco, with a forbidding exterior resembling more a prison than a palace, houses some fine religious and more general paintings. The new IP5 road, which connects the two towns, is fast and scenic.

Opposite top: Mosteiro da Batalha
Opposite below: Mondego river, Coimbra
Above: Monsanto
Below: Serra da Estrela

It is always surprising to discover the places in which early man chose to dwell. There are any number of megalithic dolmens in Beira Alta. Some are in the Castro Daire-Vila Nova de Paiva area, others in Arca, south of Vouzela, and at Fornos de Algodres. Not everyone goes overboard about the dwellings and burial grounds of our Stone and Bronze Age forbears. For many, though, the distinctive Beira domestic architecture holds great charm. Frequently the living accommodation, which is approached by an external granite staircase, is on the first floor with the ground floor providing space for domestic animals. There are also good examples of grander country houses. Two we are particularly fond of are Casa da Insua, one of the homes of the Duke of Albuquerque near Penalva do Castelo, and the less sumptuous Anadia Palace at Mangualde.

Beira Baixa

Until the pousada at Monsanto was opened at the end of 1993 there was no pousada in the lower part of Beira. It is a delightful region close to Spain with the town of Castelo Branco, famous for its embroidery, as its capital. Once again the old bishop's palace has been utilised as a museum. The Museu de Francisco Tavares

Proença Júnior, surrounded by formal gardens, not only houses an extensive collection of paintings, furniture and coins, it is also the home of a school of embroidery. Panels worked in silk (this was a great spot for silk worms) are so much in demand that the waiting list is anything up to a year. If you can persuade the director that, having reached the *Idade de Ouro* you may not be alive to enjoy their work, or indeed pay for it in a year's time, you may find her prepared to stretch a point. A gooey cake for the girl needleworkers may finally tip the scales in favour of an earlier delivery.

The interesting waterwheels, which raise water from river level to the fields above, are characteristic of the area. On the Spanish border at Monfortinho there is one of Portugal's major spas whose waters, it is claimed, benefit the health in general and the skin in particular.

Opposite top: Monsanto
Opposite below: Coimbra University's baroque library
Above and below: Monsanto

A glance at the map will explain why an approach through the town of Aveiro is not recommended. Among its considerable charms are the prettiest policewomen in Portugal. The fact that they have but a passing acquaintance with the Pousada da Ria and absolutely no idea how to get there is easily forgiven.

This pousada dips its toes into the sheltered lagoon waters of Ria de Aveiro and has been a popular retreat since it opened in 1960. It has been modernised and

further bedrooms, a swimming pool and a tennis court added. It now has 18 bedrooms and one suite which, like the reception rooms, overlook the water.

At one time the port of Aveiro was busy and prosperous, but silting up of the entrance has caused its declined. On the inland waterways the distinctive and pretty *moliceiros* with their high painted bow and stern have been partly responsible for

Aveiro's pseudonym - the Venice of Portugal. However, these boats carry, not romantic singing gondoliers, but algae which is used as a fertiliser. The town has

> **" ❝** *this pousada dips its toes into sheltered lagoon waters and has been a popular retreat since it opened* **❞**

R

19

some good classical buildings overlooking the canals.

The area is well-known for the production of ceramics. The porcelain works of Vista Alegre, renowned both in Portugal and overseas, have their headquarters and a museum near Ilhavo, a short run south. *Azulejos* are glazed tiles, so named because *azul,* meaning blue, was their predominant colour. A tourist office in Praça da República can provide a street plan and tell you the streets in which you can see good examples of the art. Rua de João Mendonça, Rua Barbosa de Magalães and Rua do Rato are three.

Exploration of the surrounding areas has been made easy by new motorways. Two excursions which suggest themselves: out on the RN 109 to Figueira da Foz; turn inland there to follow the north bank of the Mondego via Montemor-o-Velho and Tentúgal. If Aveiro is Portugal's Venice, Figueira da Foz is certainly its Blackpool.

The return can either be by the fast A1 or, if the university town of Coimbra is to be included, back on the old E50 via Anadia and Águeda. On the way home, look in at Curia, a fashionable spa still saturated with an atmosphere of the *belle époque.*

The second trip follows the north bank of the Vouga through Oliveira de Frades to Viseu. There are many things to see on this route, including some beautiful riverside scenery.

Before leaving the pousada, a tidy well-run ship with a friendly crew, compare the might of the Atlantic with the sheltered peacefulness of the lagoon.

POUSADA ACTIVITIES
Swimming, tennis, countryside bicycle tours and family games.

AREA ACTIVITIES
Shooting (duck, coot, moorhen, grouse and wood pigeon), fishing, clay pigeons, bird-watching, cruises along the Aveiro river, horse riding and mountain cycling.

HOW TO FIND
Not easy. Take the road from Aveiro going north to Estarreja. There, take the road going west to Torreira. Then go south towards S. Jacinto. After about 3kms, a track on your left leads to the pousada beside the inland water.

T his 45-room pousada was opened at the end of 1993 and has now had time to settle down into a first-rate establishment of the standard of a five-star hotel with lifts, swimming pool, terraces and tennis court.

It occupies the site of the Palácio dos Almadas dating back to the 14th century. King Manuel I is reputed to have stayed here en route to Santiago de Compostela in 1514. It was redeveloped over the centuries but razed by the French in 1811. It was in a similar state of ruin when the task of reconstructing the palace as a

pousada was undertaken. The architects are to be congratulated on the achievement. The buildings are still pristine in comparison with the shabby established charm of the older Palácio Sotto Mayor opposite. It is an extremely comfortable pousada in which an atmosphere of opulence has been created, in part by the inclusion of wall panels and other period features removed from distinguished buildings in Lisbon and elsewhere.

an extremely comfortable pousada in which an atmosphere of opulence has been created

Santa Cristina

R

45

POUSADA ACTIVITIES

Swimming, tennis and countryside bicycle tours.

AREA ACTIVITIES

Hunting, fishing (sea), cruises, rowing, rafting (Mondego river), horse riding, mountain cycling, birdwatching, traditional games and shooting.

HOW TO FIND

*No problems.
On the west side of the main road which runs parallel to the new IP1 (A1)*

There is a good terrace overlooking lawns and the swimming pool, and several bedrooms have individual terraces. The layout makes this pousada ideal for conferences or conventions.

It is convenient for visiting the major Roman ruins at Conimbriga (2 kms) and Coimbra (15 kms) where the ancient university, founded by D. Dinis in 1290, must not be missed. The library is a baroque jewel dating from 1717. At one time, undergraduates wore long black capes. Each rip in the cape represented a romantic conquest. Judging by the tattered state of these *capas* when I first saw them in the 1960's, the scholastic calendar must have been rather more erogenous than academic.

There is an interesting Casa Museu Fernando Namora nearby. In fine weather, a trip on the *Basófias* along the river Mondego is something which will give you the atmosphere of this justifiably proud part of Portugal.

Santa Cristina will always be one of our favourites.

Close to Spain, this is an area which is not much on the tourist map. Partly for that reason it has a feeling of remoteness which is accentuated in the wild and rocky Serra de Marofa. Beira Alta is not the guide compiler's favourite

hunting ground. It is a bit off the beaten track and, apart from the towns of Viseu and Guarda, does not seem to warrant their attention. *Fodor's Guide*, excellent in so many ways, doesn't even mention Almeida. More's the pity, because for many visitors this may be where the first night in Portugal is spent.

A number of the spacious bedrooms in the pousada have verandas with commanding views. The wall decorations include some valuable silk embroidery panels worked at the school in Castelo Branco. Importantly for many laden travellers, the pousada has an underground car-park.

Almeida is a fortress town but not so commercialised as many. Like most of these fortified towns, during its long history it has changed hands between the Portuguese, Spanish and French. King Dinis conquered the town in 1296 and made it part of Portugal the following year. During subsequent reigns it was extended and improved.

The present star-shaped layout owes much to that

POUSADA DE ALMEIDA

Senhora das Neves

R

21

POUSADA ACTIVITIES

Family games

AREA ACTIVITIES

Fishing (river), four-wheel driving, cruises, hot air ballooning, nature trails, countryside bicycle excursions, shooting and gymnastics.

HOW TO FIND

Easy. Inside the old and small fortress town of Almeida which lies close to the Spanish frontier west-north-west of Guarda and south-west of Pinhel.

doyen of military defences, the Frenchman Marshal Sebastien de Vauban (1633-1707). During the wars of Louis XIV he was responsible for over one hundred fortresses. Not surprisingly, his geometric star-shaped design with a surrounding moat became the accepted standard - largely because of the enfiladed artillery fire which this design allowed to be used so effectively.

Almeida is immortalised in the history of the Peninsular Wars because Wellington's forces were under siege here. Barrels of gunpowder were being transferred to the ramparts. A French shell landed close to the front doors and ignited a trail of gunpowder which had leaked from a split barrel. The gunpowder acted as a fuse running down to the main magazine in the cellars. One minute later the whole of Almeida erupted. The most violent explosion the world had seen, obliterated the town on the 26th August 1810. The cathedral and surrounding houses were reduced to rubble. It was reported that the noise of the explosion, which killed an estimated 1,300, was heard more than 50 kilometres away.

Now all is peaceful and serene. The dust has long since settled. The delightfully named pousada (Lady of the Snows) offers the traveller the opportunity of making a rendezvous with history in the comfort of a modern establishment. From the Praça de Armas you may explore these ancient walls and relive the past.

Prehistoric rock engravings in the valley of the river Côa, discovered during the construction in 1995 of a new dam, were a find of major archeological importance. The huge dam project was stopped at great expense and the site turned into the Foz Côa Archaeological Park which opened to the public in August 1996.

The building was opened in 1962 but considerable sums were spent in 1995 to modernise and refurbish this creeper-clad pousada with the result that its attraction has been much improved.

It is situated only some 50 metres from a steep road and inevitably there is

some traffic noise as vehicles in low gear fight the gradients, but the pousada has a deserved reputation and is so popular that early booking is recommended. It was full last time we tried to get a room.

Because of the climate, Caramulo was originally a sanatorium centre. Modern medicine has largely superseded its need. Of the original 18 establishments catering for victims of lung disease, most are derelict after a brief respite as

> *a perfect spot among the chestnut and mimosa trees that clothe the slopes near this well-manicured town*

R

12

POUSADA ACTIVITIES

Swimming pool and family games.

AREA ACTIVITIES

Golf and health club.

homes for returning immigrants from Portugal's former colonies. Now it is a perfect spot for a healthy holiday among the chestnut and mimosa trees that clothe the slopes near this well-manicured town.

The town has a vintage car museum housing a 1938 Rolls Royce which has carried two Popes, President Eisenhower and, in 1985, Queen Elizabeth II on a state visit to Portugal. Salazar's bullet-proof Mercedes Benz is also on show.

For no apparent reason there is a miscellaneous collection of walking sticks which, in addition to their normal function, can write, shoot or provide a home for drink, snuff and sword. There is also a good art museum, with paintings by major artists like Picasso, Chagall and Dali.

Caramulo is in the Serra do Caramulo at a modest height of 750 metres. The highest point is Caramulinho (1,074 m). On a clear day the view is magnificent with the mountains of Serra da Estrela away to the east.

It is possible you have reached Caramulo via the pousada at Oliveira do Hospital. The road via Lagares, Ervedal, Oliveira do Conde, Beijos and Tondela (N230) is a delight, although not always well signposted. Charming villages with humble picturesque cottages mingle happily with ancestral homes.

The region is interlaced with rivers and the ample water supply in these protected valleys encourages fruit and vegetable growing. The scenery is richer and greener than much of Beira Alta, where rocky and barren wastes often merge with pine forests.

São Jerónimo is a useful staging post in the midst of some beautiful countryside.

HOW TO FIND
Fairly straightforward. Caramulo is on the road from Águeda (look on your map east from Aveiro on the coast) to Tondela (south of Viseu). The pousada is situated 1km beyond the village of Caramulo, on the road to Tondela, on your left-hand side.

W ell-designed and purpose-built in 1971, several improvements have been carried out at this pousada in recent years, including the addition of an excellent swimming pool. Snacks and drinks at the pool side are an attractive feature during the summer months. The bedrooms are spacious with verandahs which, together with the principal reception rooms, overlook the lower slopes of the Serra da Estrela.

The new east-west IP5 from Guarda makes this pousada a useful stopping place en route to Gouveia, Coimbra and Lisbon. There is plenty of parking. Incidentally, the initials IP, which puzzles some travellers, stand for *Itinerário Principal*. IC stand for *Itinerário Complementar* (usually an alternative route).

The construction of these trunk roads in recent years has opened up the country and greatly added to the speed of getting from A to B. It is, however, in the minor byways that the real Portugal offers her treasures. The nearby valley of the river Alva and the ancient village of Avô, for example, are delights which should not be missed, for here you are in the true heart of Portugal. Even the Mondego, unlike many of Portugal's rivers, owes not one drop of its existence to Spain.

There is a great variety of scenery. Sheltered valleys with fruit trees, more open land with olive and cork, massive boulders in rocky outcrops, pine-clad foothills of the Serra da Estrela, elegant towns with spacious avenues, fountains and parks all jostle with hamlets. In a limited stay, one is spoilt for choice.

> *there is a great variety of scenery..... in a limited stay one is spoilt for choice*

POUSADA DE PÓVOA DAS QUARTAS

Santa Bárbara

R

16

POUSADA ACTIVITIES
Swimming pool, tennis and family games.

AREA ACTIVITIES
Shooting (rabbit, partridge, thrush and grouse), fishing (river), countryside walking and mountain bikes tours, horse riding, four-wheel driving, hot air ballooning, micro lighting, gliding, golf, canoeing, climbing, mountain tracking, four-wheel motorbikes and paintball.

HOW TO FIND
Needs care. Oliveira do Hospital lies about half-way between Coimbra and Guarda, just off the road, left. On the main road ignore the sign to Oliveira do Hospital. After 4 kms, you will come to the hamlet of Póvoa das Quartas. The pousada is on the right.

The pousada is situated in the hamlet of Povoa das Quartas some 13 kms from the town of Oliveira do Hospital. Outside the church, which has a good painted ceiling, is a statue of a medieval knight. The town probably gets its name from the Hospitallers, a religious order of knighthood who were the immensely wealthy rivals of the Knights Templar. Beginning as a hospital for pilgrims to Jerusalem during the Crusades, the order took on a more military role. The Hospitallers returned from Palestine with Henry of Burgundy, the father of Portugal's first king (Afonso Henriques 1139-1185). In more recent times they were known as the Knights Templar of Malta. The local museum is installed in the mansion of the local Cabral Metelo family.

A suggestion would be to travel north on the N230-1 to the spa at Felgueira, passing on the way some mature manor houses in very pleasant country. Then take the N234 to Mangualde to see the Palácio Anadia. If time permits, have a peep at the ghostly and deserted monastery at Maceira Dão. It is 5 kms to the west of the town and although it takes a bit of finding, it is a rewarding digression. On again north to Penalva do Castelo where one's journey ends at the nearby Casa da Insura, a splendid 18th-century mansion and one of the homes of the young and wealthy Duke of Albuquerque, whose family ancestors developed Portuguese influence in India and Malaysia. The classic mansion dates from the late 1700's and is set in well-wooded grounds. Hopefully the house will be open to the public again. A major burglary necessitated its closure. Fortunately, most of the valuables were recovered, and you are still able to enjoy the grounds.

Torre, one of the peaks not far from this pousada, rises to 2,000 metres. It is the highest point of the Serra da Estrela, the highest mountain range in Portugal. The Serra da Estrela is as different from the plains and coastal pleasures resorts as the Pyrenees are from the south of France.

Most winters, Torre gives the opportunity for skiing. Clube de Montanhismo in Covilhã or the tourist office can give further details. The area is at the centre of the national park of Serra da Estrela, a marvellous area for walking through ever-changing scenery, from the cruel, imposing, upper slopes to the wonderfully wooded lower ones. The local towns of Manteigas (originally famous for butter, as its name implies), Covilhã, Gouveia and Seia are places to be visited by car.

As the map shows, the Serra da Estrela is laced with rivers and streams, the biggest being the Mondego. Keep an eye out for the waterwheels operating on the banks to irrigate the fields at a level higher than the water. Later, dine on trout at the pousada's restaurant.

Although the pousada experiences sub-zero temperatures in winter, it has been built to withstand the elements. The external appearance conceals the warmth of the welcome inside where roaring log fires, good central heating, double glazing, wood panelling, warm blankets and curtains all combine to create a general feeling of snugness. The pousada has a terrace with breathtaking views.

The water comes from mountain springs and is nectar after a mountain hike. You may see a Serra da Estrela dog. We couldn't resist this handsome mountain breed and 'Sarah' is still with us as a loyal friend and wonderful guard dog. Wolves

POUSADA DE MANTEIGAS

São Lourenço

R

21

have been reported roaming these upper reaches, although we have never seen one. In any case, the pousada has a terrace with breathtaking views.

Poço do Inferno is a nearby waterfall, one of many in the Serra. In full flood, when the snows are melting, it crashes down the mountain with splendid force. Zêzere is supposed to be a perfect example of a glacial valley, but the rock formations at Cabeça do Urso (bear's head) and Cabeça da Velha (old lady's head) might appeal more. In fact, staring at the shapes of these craggy pinnacles, the imagination can conjure up almost anything.

The road from Seia (N321) climbs very steeply. The cross-country route via Sabugueiro (which claims to be highest village in Portugal) is not a good surface, but it has all the atmosphere of this mountain range. At frequent intervals along the roadside are two-metre high posts in orange and black bands, a reminder to the fair-weather motorist that these markers may be the only indication in winter snow and fog of the whereabouts of this mountain pass. There is a lethal drop if you get it wrong. On these roads it does not take long to realise that the passenger has more opportunity than the driver of appreciating the view.

Ornithologists come from afar to study the bird-life and it is a great place for wildflowers. The wild pansy (*viola arvensis*) is one. Collect a few. It has a lovely name in Portuguese - *amor-perfeito* - "perfect love".

There is an enormous difference between winter and summer weather - between the frightening grandeur of these freezing, sinister, misty peaks in January and the spring flowers and snow-capped friendliness of the mountains in the sunshine of May.

POUSADA ACTIVITIES

Family games, countryside walking excursions and snooker.

AREA ACTIVITIES

Fishing (trout), mountain bikes, birdwatching, handgliding, carriage tours, hot air ballooning, four-wheel driving and helicopter flying.

HOW TO FIND

Manteigas lies south-west of Guarda, south-east of Viseu and north of Covilhã. From Manteigas take the main road to Gouveia (38kms north-west) and travel for 13kms. The pousada is on the main road.

> " ... with the unpolluted air from the mountains, you would go a long way to beat the Convento de Belmonte. "

Belmonte, in Beira Baixa, is famous as the birthplace of Pedro Alvares Cabral, the celebrated Portuguese mariner who discovered Brazil in 1500. His family vaults are in a chapel near the hilltop São Tiago church although Pedro himself was buried in Santarém. Belmonte is also renowned as one of the havens where Jews congregated in an attempt to avoid the worst affects of the Spanish Inquisition. Their plight was worsened by the marriage, in 1497, of Portugal's

King Manuel to Isabel of Castile. One of the conditions of this marriage was that Portugal should rid itself of its large and growing Jewish population. The bestial *auto-da-fé* was a popular entertainment in the 16th century. Many jews, always a proud, persecuted and pragmatic race, became nominal Christians; some intermarried with Catholics. Nevertheless, they never relinquished their hearts belief and to this day there is an active Jewish community in Belmonte.

Belmonte is a fascinating town about 20kms north-east of Covilhã. As the name implies (Latin *belli monte*), it occupies a commanding hill crowned by a ruined castle (14th century) to which a number of unsuccessful restoration attempts have

H

24

POUSADA ACTIVTIES

Family games

AREA ACTIVITIES

Fishing, four wheel driving, horse riding and country walks.

HOW TO FIND
Easy. From the centre of Belmonte follow the Pousada signs.

been made in the past. Apart from the two churches, one of which contains the sculpture of Our Lady of Good Hope that reputedly accompanied Alvares Cabral on his voyage of discovery of Brazil, by far the most interesting building is the three-storied Tower of Centum Cellas. This Roman granite construction, which stands about 2 kms to the north of the town, is sufficiently intact to enable the visitor to imagine the original. None of the reference books have any real idea as to its purpose. Some say a prison, which seems unlikely in view of the sizeable windows. Others favour it as a temple. Your guess will be as good as anyone else's. That it was an important building is obvious and, for what it is worth, I would guess it to be the residence of the area's Roman military commander.

About 30 kms north of Belmonte is the sizeable town of Guarda. It is an easy journey along the IP2. At 1,057 metres it is the highest town in Portugal but it is worth making a detour to reach Torre which, at 2,000 metres, is the highest peak in the whole country. Avoid this detour in bad weather when the roads can be blocked by snow. The peak and the upper stretches of the Serra da Estrela are best left to the skiers in the winter.

As the name implies, the town guarded the frontiers of Portugal from invaders and it lacks the inspiring charm of many other Portuguese towns. Nevertheless, it is certainly worth a visit and its commanding cathedral will remind you of the better-known Batalha Abbey. This is partly because when the cathedral was completed in the 16th century the architects were the sons of the original Batalha designers.

A good place to start a tour of Guarda is the Praça de

Luis de Camões in the shade of the cathedral. The medieval town gate of Torre dos Ferreiros, close to the Bishop's Palace, can also be included in your stroll. Wander almost anywhere and you will come across arcaded walks and houses of wealthy citizens which retain the charm of the past.Some of the 16th to 18th century houses bear impressive coats of arms.

For many, however, it is the romance of the past which impresses more than the buildings. For it was here that João I had an affair with a shoemaker's daughter. Considering that João had taken a vow of chastity at the age of seven, he seems to have had a great penchant for woman christened 'Inês'. He had two children by Inês Pires, a young aristocrat, and then, in Guarda, a son by Inês Fernandes. She was the daughter of a Jewish shoemaker. How they met remains a mystery, but *A Descoberta de Portugal* claims that this child became the first Duke of Bragança. Other historians give this honour to Afonso, Inês Pires' son.

To return to the pousada, it was opened in the second half of the year 2000 and is an interesting result of government and private capital combining to restore an ancient monument. The fact that it has been put to practical use as a pousada is to the credit of all concerned. Like most convents, it has had a chequered career. Founded and funded largely by the Cabral family in the 16th century, it fell into disuse with the disestablishment of the monasteries.

In 1836 it was bought by the Count of nearby Curia and it is his descendents, together with Enatur, who have been responsible for creating this 23-bedroom pousada. Excavations have disclosed archeological finds dating back well before 1563 when the convent was founded. Much of the artefacts will be claimed by museums, but it would be of considerable interest to visitors if some of them could be displayed in the pousada as has been done at Alcácer do Sal in Alentejo.

Only 1,400 metres from the town, the pousada is simply designed on two floors with good views across the river Zêzere and its tributaries to the massive Serra da Estrela. It is a peaceful rural area with some good trout fishing. The Beiras are well-known for their cuisine and we are sure the 60-seat dining-room will establish itself as a first-class restaurant. Many of the local villages produce the popular Serra da Estrela cheese.

Nearby villages to visit include Caria with its modern Aguas Radium spa and a couple of country houses of importance. Have a run out to Paul, just over 10 kms south of Covilhã, and look out for the waterwheels on the river banks which, from Moorish times, have raised water from river level to higher fields growing cereals.

Sortelha and Sabugal to the east of Belmonte are two small fortified towns within easy reach of the pousada. They will help you to appreciate how heavily guarded was the eastern flank of Portugal.

For a restful break amid Beira's countryside, with the unpolluted air from the mountains, you would go a long way to beat the Convento de Belmonte.

This small pousada (10 rooms), opened in 1993, honours a promise. In 1938, during the Salazar regime, Monsanto was presented with a golden cockerel. It acknowledged the dictator's passion for what he considered to be the loveliest village in Portugal. "In making this award to the village of Monsanto, I wish you to ensure a pousada is built to encourage visitors." More than 60 years later, under a democratic government, the wish became a reality. A replica of the golden cockerel surmounts the clock tower.

Of the 10 rooms, two face the surrounding countryside. The others overlook the village. Room 103, with a small terrace, is the best. There is a lift and an intimate dining-room.

The wall coverings are worthy of mention. The largest is from Castelo Branco and is in delicately worked silk. These panels are not cheap and this particular one would be worth about 1,500,000 escudos. Demand outstrips supply and over the years Castelo Branco embroidery and Arraiolos carpets have proved sound and pleasurable investments.

The countryside to the south and east is more fertile and attractive than to the north where it is strewn with boulders until the Serra da Malcata is reached. This vast area is now a national park.

Monsanto is a corruption of *monte santo* (holy hill). This commanding and rocky eminence has views of Spain (20 kms) and as late as Easter the morning sun sparkles on the snow-clad upper slopes of the Serra da Estrela.

Monsanto was given by King Afonso Henriques to the Knight Templar, Gualdim Pais, in 1165. Originally a strategic castle against invaders, the subsequent centuries saw houses springing up around the military defences, some built into the rock face. Many of the cottages are hewn out of huge boulders with little pocket handkerchief gardens where chickens and primulas complete for pride of place. It really is an enchanting and unique spot.

With its fame, crowds are attracted. The height of the holiday season, when

> *this commanding and rocky eminence ...... it really is an enchanting and unique spot*

POUSADA DE MONSANTO

Monsanto

R

10

parking becomes a problem, is not the best time to enjoy the tiny alleys and minute squares. Spring or autumn, or even a good spell in winter, are ideal times to appreciate the village and its outlook. The local authority, ever mindful of the comfort of its visitors, has erected a public lavatory which must have the best views of any public lavatory in the world.

Any number of the surrounding villages have good examples of 17th and 18th century Beira houses, often decorated with coats of arms. Nearby Idanha-a-Velha should be included in your itinerary. Like Monsanto, it is a picture postcard village with great scope for the photographer. Excavations have taken place in, under and around the village church and there is a good display of Roman artefacts.

For visitors who like larger towns, Castelo Branco (45 kms) is an interesting, lively and prosperous place.

POUSADA ACTIVITIES

Family games.

AREA ACTIVITIES

Fishing, bird-watching, four-wheel driving, hot air ballooning and swimming pool.

HOW TO FIND

Easy. In the centre of this mountain village. Watch out for hairpin bends. Limited car-parking.

Sabugal
Penamacor

EN 233

MONSANTO
EN 239
Penha Garcia

Barragem Idanha-A-Velha
Idanha-A-Velha

85

R ibatejo lies to the east of Lisbon and the coastal province of Estremadura. It occupies an area of 2,550 sq. miles (6,600 sq. kms) and in the main consists of the highly fertile basin of Portugal's principle river, the Tagus. It is more densely populated on the higher ground but nothing compared to Estremadura which, of course, includes the capital city of Lisbon.

On the plains around the riverside town of Vila Franca de Xira some of Portugal's finest horses and bulls are bred. At Portuguese *touradas* you can see the authentic skill of mounted bullfighters, known as *cavaleiros,* as man and horse encircle and enrage their adversary in a highly stylised, combative spectacle. The bullfight ends with amateur *moços de forcado,* with considerable skill and matching bravery, bringing the bull to a standstill with their bare hands. The bull is not killed as in other countries and whether you are a devotee of the sport or loathe it, you have to admire the skill of horse and man as they combine in a ritualistic pageant which goes back to Roman and Greek times. Etruscan pottery often depicted bullfighting scenes, which are re-enacted today in the rings of Ribatejo. The Ribeiro Telles family, from their Ribatejo estate at Coruche, have done much to promote and prolong the popularity of this artistic but controversial sport. Despite their attempts, though, the youth of Portugal

The Province of Ribatejo

> *Ribatejo is synonymous with cattle and bullfighting*

are increasingly deserting the bullring for the soccer stadium. Nevertheless, tradition dies hard and the fairs and festivals from Easter onwards are often centred around the bullfight. The festival of the *colete encarnado* (red vest), when the bulls run loose through the streets of Vila Franca, is as popular today as ever and a reason - or perhaps an excuse - for much merriment and prodigious wining and dining.

Although Ribatejo is synonymous with cattle and bullfighting, there are great stretches of salt flats bordering the Tagus and its tributaries. The marshy land is also ideal for growing bamboo and osier, much used in basketwork.

The only pousada in Ribatejo is at Castelo de Bode, south of the ancient town of Tomar and not far from the island of Almourol. Castles also surmount the towns of Abrantes and the provincial capital, Santarém. Many of the houses in these low-lying districts are periodically flooded and some, like the impressive home of the Duke of Cadaval at Muge, have the height of earlier flood levels marked on their walls.

A visit to Alpiarça, north of Almeirin, gives the visitor the opportunity of inspecting the house of José Relvas, a successful politician at the turn of the century. Now a museum, Casa dos Patudos provides an interesting and intimate peep into the home of the wealthy.

Ribatejo is prolific in bird-life and part is designated as a sanctuary. Egrets, herons, snipe, sandpipers and many other waders are plentiful.

Opposite top: Almourol Castle
Top: Festive riding
Below: A corner of Tomar Castle

One of the great country estates in these parts is Quinta da Cardiga near Golegã. It dates back to the days of the Knights Templar and produces wine, olive oil, butter and cheese - but it is for the bull that Ribatejo is really famous.

In Beira Litoral between Santarém and Leiria, Conde de Ourém has the distinction of being the first pousada to be opened in the 21st century. It is another successful conversion of a medieval building on a very commanding site. Quite apart from providing interesting accommodation for the visitor, it is always satisfying to see these ancient monuments saved from further deterioration.

The pousada is a 16th century former hospital built by the 10th Conde (count) of Ourém. The fourth Conde was the illegitimate son of D. João I, who married Philippa of Lancaster, and the nephew of the great military leader Nuno Álvares of Aljubarrota fame. You may see his tomb in the impressive crypt of the church adjacent to the pousada. Queen Mécia Lopez, wife of King Sancho II (1223-1248), was reputedly held hostage here by a number of barons who captured her at Coimbra. Whatever the truth of past deeds, the whole area is steeped in the history of Portugal. If you stay here, you are wonderfully well-placed to acquaint yourself with some of the outstanding happenings of years gone by.

Tomar to the east and Batalha to the west are two of the great treasures, not only of Portugal, but of the whole of the Iberian peninsula. You must make time to see them both. A few more details are given in the chapters on the Batalha pousada and on São Pedro. I never tire of seeing both of these masterpieces and each time there is more to learn. Tiny markings on the flagstones of Batalha Abbey intrigued me. I had never noticed them before. They are individual marks of masons who laid them centuries ago. The foreman totalled them up

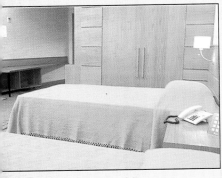

> **if you stay here you are wonderfully well-placed to acquaint yourself with some outstanding happenings of years gone by**

and the masons were paid accordingly.

As the Conde de Ourém pousada becomes established and matures, there will be more to comment upon, but, meantime, the superb views of the surrounding countryside will remain immutable. It is just over five kilometres from Fátima. This religious site is visited yearly by hundreds of thousands who find comfort in its mystical powers where three young children saw visions of the Virgin Mary. Often referred to as the "Lourdes of Portugal", it is much commercialised and may incline the agnostic to greater cynicism. The singing during the candlelight procession on the 13th May and 13th October is very impressive, whatever your belief. The millennium year saw a further visit to Fátima by Pope John Paul II during which he renewed his friendship with Lucia, aged 93, the only survivor of the original three seers.

A Gothic fountain erected by Dom Afonso bears his coat of arms and the date 1434. The town of Ourém has little to commend it, but a short journey north to the small ancient country town of Alvaiázere provides more interest. Apart from a splendid modern bandstand, there are traces of former Roman and Moorish occupation. There are blacksmiths and tinsmiths whose ancestors have plied their craft here for centuries. There are several 17th century manor houses, both in the town and surrounding villages, emblazoned with coats of arms of past nobility. Even the villages have romantic-sounding names. Stand in the alleyways of Maçãs de Caminho or Maçãs de Dona Maria and absorb the atmosphere of this tranquil and historic area.

R

30

POUSADA ACTIVITIES

Swimming pool, family games.

AREA ACTIVITIES

Country walks.

HOW TO FIND

Easy. Within the walled town of Ourém, roughly midway between Leiria and Tomar on the EN113.

As with many of the pousadas overlooking artificial lakes (*barragens*), the attractive São Pedro pousada is a conversion of the original engineer's offices. The damming of the river Zêzere was carried out between 1946 and 1952 and forms the largest artificial lake in Portugal. Unfortunately, the buildings are on the river side of the dam. A major remodelling of the existing buildings was undertaken and Pousada São Pedro reopened in 1993. It is a very quiet and comfortable pousada with a friendly and courteous staff, most of whom were working there before the reconstruction.

Tomar is the magnet that draws visitors to São Pedro. Along with Alcobaça, Batalha, and Jerónimos, the Convent of Christ at Tomar is one of the wonders of Portuguese ecclesiastical architecture. Don't miss any of them.

The town of Tomar owed its popularity to the Knights Templar who drove out the Moors. The order was dissolved by the Pope, but King Dinis (1279-1325) then founded the Order of Christ. The huge Convent of Christ dominates the town. Prince Henry the Navigator became Grand Master of the Order

> *Tomar, one of the wonders of Portuguese ecclesiastical architecture, is the magnet that draws visitors to São Pedro*

R

25

and was responsible in the early 1400's for much of the present building. The wealth of the Order helped him plan the exploration of the oceans by caravels which carried the cross of the order on their sails. A guided tour is helpful in appreciating the many styles of architecture - Moorish, Byzantine, Manueline, Gothic and Renaissance all mingle happily.

Despite repeated sackings during the Napoleonic invasions, the Templar's rotunda has survived. Octagonal-shaped, it is a 12th-century model of the Sepulchre in Jerusalem. The central window is a masterpiece. It illustrates more readily than words what is meant by Manueline architecture. The cross of the Order of Christ surmounts the royal coat of arms. There is a mass of oak trees (whose wood served to build the caravels), rope-work, seaweed, coral, chains, globes and garters (from the English Order of the Garter). To some it is fussy and overpowering, but whatever your taste, it is a masterpiece in stone by an unknown genius. You will never forget it.

Every third year in July, Tomar stages the Festa dos Tabuleiros, a festival of thanksgiving where the produce is distributed to the poor. The *tabuleiro* (tray), piled high with loaves, flowers, wheat and other goodies must be as high as the person offering it. The trays are carried on the heads of the maidens of Tomar. Dressed in white, they are escorted by their menfolk. Tomar is in fiesta and continuing a tradition of great antiquity. The tables in the dining-room used to have a *tabuleiro* centrepiece.

The lake may be explored by rowing or motor boat, or by a larger vessel named the *São Cristovão*. The romantic Almourol castle in the river Tagus, south of the pousada, is a much photographed fairytale.

POUSADA ACTIVITIES

Family games.

AREA ACTIVITIES

Fishing (lake), country walks, cruises and horse riding.

HOW TO FIND

Fairly easy. Tomar is the nearest major town. Look for the small town of Constância (30kms south-east of Tomar). The pousada is where the Tomar-Constância road goes close to the barragem (lake) about 3kms from Martinchel (a village off the main road).

This is Portugal's most densely populated province and the nerve centre of the country. The visitor could spend a three-week holiday within its boundaries and not be bored nor, indeed, see everything Estremadura has to offer. It includes, of course, the city of Lisbon (Lisboa), one of Europe's loveliest and cheapest capitals, and the sizeable industrial port of Setúbal. There are four pousadas covering the 11,430 sq km (4413 sq. miles) of the province.

There is some good coastal scenery of great variety ranging from the wild and rugged capes around Peniche to the pleasure beaches of Nazaré, Ericeira, the

The Province of Estremadura

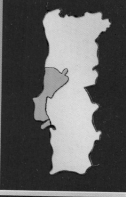

> ❝ *there is a wide choice for the holidaymaker ...... it includes the city of Lisbon, one of Europe's loveliest and cheapest capitals* ❞

sheltered waters of S. Martinho do Porto, and the Lisbon beaches of Estoril and Cascais. There is a wide choice for the holidaymaker. From the industrial heartland around Setúbal, to the fertile fruit and vegetable-growing acres near Torres Vedras; from the verdant slopes of Arrábida and Sintra, to the massive, rocky outcrops of the centre - there is this wide range of contrasting choice.

Top: Quinta do Bacalhau / Azeitão
Centre: Tróia
Below: Belém Tower

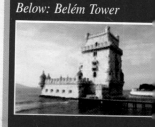

Then there are the magnificent palaces of Queluz, Ajuda and Sintra; the great monasteries of Alcobaça, Batalha, Jerónimos and Mafra; the ancient castles of Porto de Mós, Torres Vedras, Alenquer, Óbidos, Palmela and Setúbal (the last three converted into pousadas). Each is within a morning's car ride.

There are well-equipped modern spas at Vimeiro, Caldas da Rainha and Cucos, fossilized dinosaurs' footprints at Espichel, traces of early man and the caves of Zambujal. Two of Portugal's great rivers, the Tagus and the Sado, reach the Atlantic within the boundaries of Estremadura. The low-lying regions adjoining these great estuaries encourage prolific bird-life and give the visitor a chance to study the precarious nesting habits of the stork. The area also provides ideal conditions for salt-flats and rice-fields.

The colourful fishing fleets of Sesimbra and Nazaré ride at anchor alongside quayside fish restaurants. There is plenty of good wine to wash down your choice of food. The area around Colares and Sintra was spared the devastating phylloxera bug which destroyed much of Europe's best vineyards in the 1870s and 1880s.

For students of history, this is the land where Wellington proved he was one too many for the likes of Junot who commanded the French armies. The not uncommon

blond inhabitants around Vimeiro and Torres Vedras confirm the British army's success in other directions.

At present there is no pousada in Lisbon although ENATUR own a well-established restaurant in St George's Castle, an excellent vantage point from which to view the city. It is outside the scope of this book to extol the virtues of the capital, but there are many guide books on the subject. Were I to be asked to list the *musts* of a fleeting visit to the capital, I would say a view of the city's skyline from the ferry plaving between Black Horse Square and Cacilhas; a drink at a cafe on the Avenida da Liberdade; a taxi ride to include Alfama and Graça; a visit to the Coach Museum or the Gulbenkian centre; São Carlos Opera House and, finally, another drink on the Avenida da Liberdade.

Above and opposite top left: Palmela pousada
Below and opposite bottom: São Jorge Castle, Lisbon
Page 92 and opposite top right: Óbidos pousada
Page 93: Fishing cove near Peniche

a marvellous spot at which to learn a little history and appreciate architectural splendour in comfort

POUSADA
DA BATALHA

Mestre
Afonso
Domingues

R

21

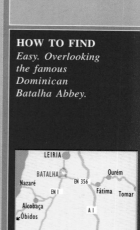

Previously a modern inn, the operation has been run as a pousada since January 1985. It is comfortable and well appointed with 20 bedrooms and one suite. Try to get a bedroom overlooking the adjoining abbey. The pousada takes its name from the architect commissioned to build the abbey by King João I. To enjoy the area with its great buildings and traditions, it is desirable to have an idea, however sketchy, of Portuguese history.

On the 1st November 1386 a marriage was arranged between King João of Portugal and Philippa of Lancaster (Edward III's granddaughter of John of Gaunt). It was, in fact, part of a package deal. King João, then 30 years old, had the choice of two daughters - Catherine, aged 14, or Philippa aged 26. Their father (John of Gaunt) promised continuing support in João's fight against the Spanish. There was a slight complication in that João had taken an oath of chastity from the age of seven, but with papal dispensation they were married in Oporto on 14th February 1387.

In the same year, a defence and commercial agreement was signed by King João's ambassador at Windsor. The Treaty of Windsor, as it became known, has survived to this day and is the longest enduring treaty in history. Of course, the liaison between Portugal and England had already been going on informally for some considerable time, with the mutual desire of defeating Spain. In August 1385, a year before the marriage arrangement, a small contingent of English archers helped João to his brilliant defeat of a Spanish army five times the size of the Portuguese force. It was during this Battle of Aljubarrota, which ensured

independence from Spain for two hundred years, that the King vowed to erect an abbey worthy of the occasion if he survived and won. Batalha (Battle) Abbey is the result. In it lie João, Philippa and their four sons, one of whom was the great Henry the Navigator who was instrumental in Portugal's success in opening sea routes to Africa, India and South America. *(See pousada Infante Sagres)*

20 kms to the south is another architectural masterpiece, the Cistercian Abbey of Santa Maria de Alcobaça. Started in 1148 by D. Afonso Henriques, the first king of Portugal, it is older than Batalha. Both commemorate victory over

invaders: Batalha over the Spanish and Alcobaça over the Moors at Santarém in 1147. Both have been extensively altered over the centuries, resulting in Manueline and Renaissance architecture being married quite successfully with the original Gothic. The aesthetic merits of one abbey over the other provide a source for endless discussion. Some are persuaded that the scales are dipped in favour of Alcobaça. Not only has the building itself a magic; it has a spell over it. The story of King Pedro and his lover, Inês de Castro, who are buried here, must be one of the most passionate pieces of legendary history ever recorded.

After succeeding his father and exacting a horrible revenge on advisors who had murdered Inês, King Pedro had her body exhumed. He commanded that her corpse be crowned and ordered his courtiers to kiss her long lifeless hand. King Pedro and Inês lie in facing tombs so that on Judgement Day they might awake to the sight of each other's eyes.

On the way to Alcobaça you can pass the battlefield of Aljubarrota and the chapel of São Jorge where a pitcher of water is available for the traveller as a reminder of the thirst suffered by the troops on that scorching day in August over 600 years ago.

Fátima (20 kms), the Lourdes of Portugal, stands on the site where three peasant children had a vision on 13th May 1917. They claimed the Virgin Mary appeared in an oak tree after a bright light in the sky. On 13th October of the same year, a further apparition was witnessed - the last one to date. The commemoration on 13th May and 13th October each year attracts up to a million pilgrims. The candlelight procession and singing create lasting memories. Pope John Paul II gave thanks to Our Lady of Fátima for his deliverance after an assassination attempt in Italy, only to survive another attempt here. He made his third visit to Fátima to beatify two of the seers on 13th May 2000.

Pousada Mestre Domingues is a marvellous spot at which to learn a little history and appreciate architectural splendour in comfort. The countryside around is restful with the production of fruit and vegetables. The grottoes of Santo António (10 kms) make a refreshing change after a surfeit of ecclesiastical architecture.

the popularity of both the town and its pousada makes the nine bedrooms totally inadequate for the demand

This early pousada, opened in 1951, is within the castle which has been much modified since Moorish times. In 1282, King Dinis gave the town to his eight-year-old wife, Isabel of Aragon. From that day to this, Óbidos has been a great favourite with the ladies. Three of the nine bedrooms are in tower suites and these are very popular with honeymooning couples.

The town is a national monument and the popularity both of the town and its pousada makes the nine bedrooms totally inadequate for the demand. It is essential to make a reservation well ahead and advisable, if possible, to avoid the very busy summer months.

The entrance, and a pair of adjoining windows to our left, are good examples of Manueline architecture. Perhaps the accommodation lacks the grandeur associated with the castles of Estremoz and Palmela, but what it lacks in size is compensated for by a friendly and informal intimacy. On the left of the reception vestibule is a small sitting-room and adjoining bar. The sitting-room sports a knight in shining armour which sets the scene. There are some good pieces of furniture and tapestries here and on the first floor where the dining-room is located.

Another royal couple who married at the castle were Afonso V and his cousin bride. Like Dinis' wife, she was an Isabella. Queen Leonor, wife of João II and Afonso's daughter-in-law, lived here. Not a happy time for her. Her son and heir

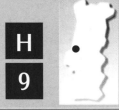

H
9

POUSADA ACTIVITIES

Family games.

AREA ACTIVITIES

Shooting, fishing, water-sports, cruises, rowing (sea and lagoon), carriage tours, horse riding and golf.

HOW TO FIND
Very easy. In the small town itself.

was killed in 1491 on returning from hunting. His body came ashore in a fisherman's net. The pillory in the church square includes in its emblem a fisherman's net so that today we are reminded of that sad event 500 years ago.

Caldas da Rainha (Queen's spa) was founded by D. Leonor. Legend has it that while en route from Óbidos to Batalha she saw a group of peasants bathing in some pretty foul-smelling water which, they claimed, possessed mystical curative powers. They were so convincing that the Queen had a dip, was cured of her ills (unspecified) and donated her jewellery for the establishment of what today is the Hospital Termal Rainha D. Leonor.

Caldas has always been popular as a creative centre and many of Portugal's most famous writers, artists and potters have lived here. The 19th-century painter José Malhôa has a museum named after him in Carlos Park. His portrait of Miss Laura Sauvinet is exquisite.

Of the nearby seaside spots, S. Martinho do Porto is a safe natural harbour and supposed to be famous for its blue shells. It took us over half-an-hour to discover one.

Despite its strongly fortified ramparts that once commanded the open sea and a bay which has long since silted up, there is something subtly feminine about Óbidos, with its cobbled streets, tiny *travessas* and whitewashed cottages. From the moment of your arrival at the galleried gateway, you will feel a welcoming atmosphere as you pass under its shady arches. This gateway is a gem, with a small oratory chapel flanked by charming 18th-century blue and white *azulejos*.

Queluz, on the western outskirts of Lisbon, is about 13 kms from the city centre. It is arguable whether a hotel in the city centre is the place to stay to explore the capital. If you find the bustle and traffic roar of a metropolis to your liking, there are any number of good hotels available. If, on the other hand, you enjoy exploring the sights and sounds of Lisbon but prefer to escape to a quieter atmosphere at the end of what can be a tiring day, then Queluz is for you. The communications to the centre are excellent. There is a good motorway and plenty of taxis which are still cheaper than in other European capitals. There are also train and bus connections.

This very plush pousada was opened in 1995. It forms part of the Queluz National Palace and is a conversion of outbuildings known formerly as the Torre do Relógio (clock tower). The palace was built in the second half of the 18th century by King Pedro III (then a prince) who married his niece (Queen Maria I). She was a devout catholic who sadly developed religious mania and died here. The conversion provides 24 bedrooms and two suites.

The achievement of ENATUR and architects Mendes and Carlos Ramos is to be admired. It compares well with the brilliance of Mateus Vicente de Oliveira and the Frenchman Robillon, who were the original creators of the palace and gardens. There is a lift to the bedrooms on the first floor. They and the public rooms on the ground floor, which include a small theatre, have been

> *this very plush pousada forms part of the Queluz National Palace*

Dona Maria I

H

26

decorated regardless of cost. The friezes and panel-ling, in 18th-century design, have been hand-painted and one can only hope that artists of similar quality are around when, eventually, redecoration is necessary. The dining-room is the long-established 'Cozinha Velha' just across the courtyard in the main palace buildings. Adjoining it is the smaller 'Sala Dourada', beautifully furnished and decorated, ideal for groups, private parties and social gatherings of one sort or another. It opens on to a terrace overlooking the palace grounds. It is a magnificent setting in summer, but it can be a bit of an excursion on a wet and windy winter's night.

The 'Cozinha velha' was originally part of the royal kitchens and the food is of a very high standard, similar to that served in the palace itself where foreign dignitaries are often hosted.

Queluz Palace is open to the public and there are other palaces to see at Sintra and Ajuda. Deciding what not to see is the real problem.

POUSADA ACTIVITIES

Guided tours to the Palace and family games.

AREA ACTIVITIES

Golf, beaches, Casino, four-wheel driving, four-wheel motorbikes and karting.

HOW TO FIND
Very easy. The pousada is located 5kms from Lisbon, in front of the National Queluz Palace, in the building of the Clock Tower.

A publicity leaflet from reception describes Palmela as being five leagues to the southeast of Lisbon. If you are none the wiser, it may help you to know it is about 40 kilometres south of the Tagus bridge, just to the right of the motorway on a turn-off that is clearly marked. The countryside skirting the motorway is flat and surprising sandy. It is only as Palmela is approached that the land rises steeply from sea-level. Palmela, founded in ancient times, probably got its name from the Latin word meaning palm leaf or victory.

Nearly 250 metres above sea-level, this converted fortress occupies a commanding and virtually unassailable position. The steep approach is up a good tarmac road with one hairpin bend to the left, which may require a couple of bites depending on the lock of your car. Once up, there is plenty of secure car

POUSADA
DE PALMELA

H
28

parking and exceptional views which, with a map, enable the visitor to get a very good idea of the lie of the land - and the sea for that matter.

The origins of the Castle of Palmela are obscured by the mists of time, but we know it was taken from the Moors in the middle of the 12th century. In the 13th century it was the headquarters of the Portuguese Knights of St James. It was extensively damaged in the earthquake of 1755, which destroyed much of Lisbon, and finally abandoned in the middle of the 19th century. After substantial reconstruction works,

POUSADA ACTIVITIES

Family games.

AREA ACTIVITIES

Cruises on the river Sado, country walks, mountain bike tours, four-wheel driving, horse riding, hot air ballooning, micro lighting, diving, canoeing, paintball, golf, karting and dolphin watching.

HOW TO FIND

Easy. If you find Palmela you cannot miss the pousada. Palmela lies just off the motorway from Setúbal to Lisbon, about 8km from Setúbal.

it was opened as a pousada in 1979. It provides 28 bedrooms and two suites. It incorporates the modern (there is a lift) while cleverly preserving the atmosphere of the ancient. The cloisters have been glassed in, as they have in dos Lóios at Évora, and provide a charming sitting-out area where drinks may be served from the adjoining bar. The wisteria-clad courtyard is also used in fine weather.

As you might expect in a pousada which has hosted the President of France and the Queen of Denmark, the food is good.

There is an ample, supporting wine list. Palmela is famous for its September wine festival (*festa das vindimas*) when great barrels of wine are paraded through the streets and children in traditional dress help to tread the grapes. The local Fonseca wines are always reliable, but if you can get hold of a bottle of 'Pedras Negras' (black stones), you have a very drinkable full-blooded red from Palmela itself.

The adjoining Serra da Arrábida is a wonderful area for wild flowers. In the spring, walking over the hills is a journey of discovery. Within 5 kms of Palmela is the hamlet of Quinta do Anjo where excavations have revealed Neolithic burial grounds dating back 5,000 years. The other road from Palmela leads to Marateca via Pinhal Novo and Rio Frio where the Palácio de Santos Jorge is located. Find time to visit Vila Fresca de Azeitão and have a look at the privately owned Quinta da Bacalhoa (15th-century), and near Vila Nogueira the Quinta das Torres (16th-century) and the Palácio of the Dukes of Aveiro (16th-century). Industrial development is invading the doorsteps of these fine old buildings; ugly mongrels snapping at the fading robes of royalty.

Some say the castle is haunted. Even though you may not encounter the ghost, remember João II (1481-95) had the Duke of Bragança, the Duke of Viseu and the Bishop of Évora done to death here. It is doubtful whether these three gentlemen would agree with the King's sobriquet - 'The Perfect Prince'.

The pousada is also an excellent base for a golfing holiday. There are now four stimulating and varied courses within easy reach, all south of Lisbon. The two closest are at Montado, and at Tróia. ENATUR have special golf packages available.

"the superb and commanding position gives views across the sea and surrounding Serra da Arrábida"

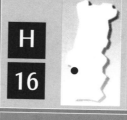

H

16

This pousada is not for the infirm or faint-hearted. Forty well-worn steps lead from the car park to reception and there are more steps to the dining-room and bedrooms. There is no lift. Providence, rather than architectural design, has strategically located a little chapel two-thirds of the way up the route march from the car park. Here one may offer thanks for a mission so far safely accomplished and seek courage and determination to achieve the final destination sound in wind and limb.

The pousada was constructed about 40 years ago in a part of the 16th-century St Philip's Castle, which was built on the orders of Philip II of Spain (Philip I of Portugal) who employed the military architect Filipo Terzi. The fortress was largely intended to thwart any possible attack from the English who had greatly damaged the king's reputation, self-confidence and prestige by the defeat of his Spanish Armada. The superb and commanding position gives views across the sea and surrounding Serra da Arrábida, a mountain range protecting the bay of Setúbal and the mouth of the River Sado. The government has learned much since this early conversion. São Filipe has a rambling layout on different levels. But what makes the place is the terrace. What a view! Here, under a sunshade, with a drink at hand and this 360° panorama, it would be surprising if the disadvantages of a little extra perambulating between floors did not evaporate.

José Maria da Fonseca produce some good wines from their winery at nearby Azeitão. 'Periquita', 'Pasmados', 'Camarate', 'Terras Altas' and 'Tinto Velho' in the reds, and 'BSE' and 'João Pires' in the whites are

POUSADA ACTIVITIES

Snooker and family games.

AREA ACTIVITIES

Shooting (hare, rabbit, partridge and quail), golf, water sports, fishing, diving, four-wheel driving, four-wheel motorbikes, micro lighting, hot air ballooning, paintball, cruises in typical boats on the river Sado and dolphin watching.

HOW TO FIND

Easy. The pousada is in part of the ancient St. Philip's Castle. Approach via Av. Luisa Tody, the road which leads to Figueirinha.

thoroughly recommended. The last named is a little too sweet for some palates and is more expensive. It makes a good dessert wine and leads naturally to a taste of the famous 'Moscatel de Setúbal'. Again, you may find this rather sweet, but you should sip a chilled five-year-old on the terrace before a meal, or try a 25-year-old after dinner. It may change your opinion of sweet wines.

Setúbal is Portugal´s fourth largest town and, after Lisbon and Oporto, the third largest port. It is, therefore, a busy industrial centre with the extensive Setenave shipyards, a major employer of local labour. Don't let the industrial nature of the town put you off. The Church of Jesus explains visually what Manueline architecture is. Late Gothic, the rope-like columns reflect Portugal´s maritime supremacy at the time. Even if you are not over keen on 16th-century religious paintings, there are other things to see in the adjoining museum, including nostalgic memorabilia of the poet Bocage (1765-1805), and Luisa Tody (1754-1833), an internationally renowned opera star. Both were born in the town.

The town produces salt from the Sado estuary and is famous for its moscatel grapes, rice, oranges and fish. There are regular ferries across the bay to Tróia, believed to be the site of the Roman Cetobriga or an even earlier Phoenician settlement. Tróia has been extensively developed as a tourist and conference complex. The unimaginative 'rent-collecting boxes' would do little to impress the Roman and Phoenician architects of the past.

Although São Filipe is smaller than the neighbouring Palmela pousada, many visitors find it more friendly and relaxing.

Before leaving, have a more detailed look at the walls of the chapel. The *azulejos* depict the life of St. Philip and are by Policarpo de Bernardes and dated 1736.

As with the pousada at Palmela, it is ideal for a golfing holiday. Two courses are only 10 kms away (Montado and Tróia) and two more a little further afield. The courses offer a good variety of golf, from the famous links course at Tróia to the parkland settings of the others.

The Upper Alentejo differs from the southern part of the province in several ways. It has no access to the sea and lacks the spectacular beaches which run from below Sines to the Algarvian border. Its western boundary is formed by the provinces of Ribatejo and Estremadura. It is more undulating and varied in landscape, with the forested mountain ranges of Ossa (653 m) and São Mamede (1025 m) offering a complete contrast to the giant cereal-growing plains further south. There is even more evidence of previous civilisations, going way

The Province of Upper Alentejo

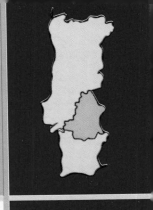

undulating and varied in landscape, with forested mountain ranges offering a complete contrast to the plains further south "

back to the Stone Age, and many well-preserved remains from the occupation by the Romans. The numerous fortified towns and isolated forts along the eastern boundary remind us that, having got rid of the Moors, the Portuguese were in constant conflict with the Spanish.

Along with the lower part of the province and

Top: Traditional handicrafts
Below: Marble quarry

113

despite its more undulating and varied landscape, this is the country's principle cereal-producing region, with olives, pines, chestnuts, eucalyptus, cork oaks and cattle all providing income to a province which has not always been prosperous. Major irrigation schemes and land reforms following the 1974 revolution have done much to improve conditions.

Local arts and crafts are similar to the Lower Alentejo, but it is with the needle

that the womenfolk of Alto Alentejo have left an indelible mark. The gros point Arraiolos carpets, the modern petit point panels of Portalegre and the crochet and applique work from Nisa are craftsmanship of a very high standard. Pottery, marble and wines are all first-rate products of these areas.

The main towns are Évora, Estremoz, Elvas and Portalegre. All have pousadas within the fortress walls or nearby. It was here in the Alentejo that royal weddings took place and many a proposed liaison was the forerunner of attempts to merge the thrones of Portugal, France and Spain. None of them proved to be permanently successful.

At Vila Viçosa there is a gigantic royal palace next to which, in the Convento das Chagas de Cristo, a pousada has been constructed.

Page 112 top: Estremoz
Page 112-113 bottom: Évora

Opposite top: Megalithic chapel at Pavia
Opposite bottom: Castelo de Vide

Above: Temple of Diana in front of the Pousada

The location of the most northerly of the Alentejo pousadas is far removed in character from the open plains normally associated with this province. Marvão is a fortified mountain stronghold reminiscent of Óbidos, but on a smaller scale and not so commercialised. Close to the Spanish border, it has been a fortress since Roman times. Some of the 13th-century walls and ramparts remain with some 17th-century modifications, and many Roman artefacts have been found locally.

The pousada was converted from two private houses in 1976 when it had eight bedrooms. Its increasing popularity justified major reconstruction which was completed in 1992. There are now 29 bedrooms. The dining-room is a real 'roof-top rendezvous'. Splendid views and splendid food are an ideal combination. Add to this good wine and attentive service, and all the ingredients for a memorable time are at hand. It is quite a climb up to Marvão, but business people from nearby towns find it worthwhile. Combined with visitors, they make the restaurant surprisingly busy.

A pleasant hour or so may be spent in the adjoining

POUSADA DE MARVÃO

Santa Maria

R

29

bar, studying the menu or picking out landmarks from your map - Serra da Estrela to the north (Portugal's highest mountain range), Serra de São Mamede to the south and west, and the neighbouring Spanish plains in the east.

The nearby convent of Nossa Senhora da Estrela (Our Lady of the Star), founded in 1448, is supported, as the inscription says, by 'Love and Faith'. Ten sisters care for handicapped children and geriatrics. The little chapel off the cloisters has a substantial weighing-machine on which offerings of grain can be weighed. The convent is not officially open to the public, but a donation to such a worthy cause can open many doors.

There is a helpful tourist office in the nearby spa town of Castelo de Vide, which will suggest a walk around the interesting parts of the town. A charming legend explains how the town got its name (Castle of the Vine). The ravishing Guiomar loved Martim Gil. Guiomar's father did not and wanted her to marry someone else. The young lovers eloped to Martim's castle where they planted a vine and called the place 'Terra de Vide' (Land of the Vine). The King ordered the couple to fortify, develop and defend the holding. As the town grew and the castle was enlarged, it became Castelo de Vide (Castle of the Vine). As if to authenticate the story, the vine forms part of the town's coat of arms. The old part of the town and the former Jewish quarters are a delight. Have a look at the tiny synagogue and the 16th-century marble fountain.

At the foot of the impregnable battlement of Marvão there is some enjoyable countryside with groves of chestnut and walnut trees. The distance on the signposts are often 'approx' - time and distance have low priorities in these parts.

POUSADA ACTIVITIES

Family games.

AREA ACTIVITIES

Shooting, fishing (dam), golf, theme tours, country walks, cycling, cruises, horse riding, carriage tours, four-wheel driving, mountain bikes, canoeing, diving, bird watching, skating and picnics.

HOW TO FIND

Easy. In the village of Marvão itself not far from the 13th-century fortress remains.

The pousada occupies a busy position on the edge of the town. There has been a hostelry on this site for more than 50 years. It was acquired by the government and opened as a pousada in the mid-1970's. It provides a useful stopover en route between Spain and Portugal, and a good centre from which to explore the upper Alentejo.

Elvas is a busy, bustling border town with good shopping. From the pousada you can see the gigantic Amoreiras aqueduct, with its 843 arches, which was built on Roman foundations between 1529 and 1622. It took so long because, like many of today's projects, there was a shortage of funds. The fountain of São Lourenço was constructed soon after. Also in the town are good examples of wrought-iron work and the opportunity of seeing craftsmen working in copper. The town has a fascinating atmosphere created partly by its ancient past and partly by its absorption of Spanish influences.

To many travellers crossing the frontier from Badajoz (18 kms), this will be their first encounter with Portugal. To others it will be a return home to a country with familiar sounds and scents, and meals at more civilised times. Remember to check the time; there can be an hour's difference.

These frontier towns are now prosperous and peaceful, with little evidence of the xenophobia which plagued their past. Alandroal, Terena and Monsaraz are three other fortified towns worthy of a visit. Of course, the jewel in the

R

25

POUSADA ACTIVITIES

*Pool, tennis and
family games.*

AREA ACTIVITIES

*Shooting , fishing
and horse riding*

HOW TO FIND

*Easy. In the old town
which is reached by
turning left off the main
road to Badajoz and
Spain, going under the
famous aqueduct and
climbing the hill. Once
there, everyone knows
where the pousada is if
you miss the sign.*

crown of these parts is the Palace of Vila Viçosa (18 kms). A pousada has been constructed next to the Palace.

The Palace, started in 1500 and completed in the 17th century, became a favourite royal residence of the Braganças who ruled from 1640 to the end of the monarchy in 1910. Catherine of Bragança was born here in 1638. Her marriage to Charles II of England would have altered history if she had had children. Although he had none by his wife, Charles had many from his various mistresses. He had sons who became the Dukes of Monmouth, Southampton, Grafton, Richmond, and St Albans (Nell Gwynn's boy).

The guided tours around the palace were not well-organised when we last visited and foreigners had difficulty in following the Portuguese dialogue. Hopefully this problem will be overcome and the many foreign visitors will be able to get some idea of what is going on. We would recommend reading your guide book beforehand.

Carlos I, the penultimate Bragança monarch, spent his last day here with his son before they were both assassinated in the streets of Lisbon in 1908. An amateur artist, his work is competent and appealing.

To some, the Bragança Palace is a boring, uninspired monster. To others it is a powerful and dominating classic in which Portugal's history is enshrined. Whatever its effect on you, you will return to the Santa Luzia pousada with an appetite. We have never had a bad meal in the pousada restaurant; some have been memorable.

Housed in a new building, this pousada was inaugurated in 1992 by the then prime minister, Prof. Anibal Cavaco Silva. It was an interesting development by ENATUR and local businessmen who combined to form ENASEL to promote country pursuits like shooting and fishing. The pousada stands in fine countryside and is well-equipped with kennels, cleaning rooms, gun and storage facilities to provide for these sports.

You may be assured that if local dignitaries interested in hunting are involved, the food will be good. Certainly the Sunday buffet lunch is a banquet by any standard. The last time we were there the menu included 19 different dishes. The accent was naturally on local game and fish.

The pousada occupies a commanding position on a hilltop 3 kms from the country town of Sousel and about 20 kms from Estremoz. There are 28 double bedrooms, four suits and a restaurant seating 200. If you are keen on shooting, or coarse fishing on the Maranhão dam, you will find the management most helpful.

A minute and ancient bullring adjoins the pousada. Each Easter Monday it is

> *the pousada stands in fine countryside and is well equipped for country pursuits like shooting and fishing*

a scene of great festivity in honour of Nossa Senhora do Carmo da Serra. It is the only day on which the bullring is used. I am reliably informed that it was the first bullring ever built in Portugal. Cabeço de Vide (20 kms) is a small spa town with a railway station which would easily win the award for the most prolific *azulejos* tiling. The

panels depict country life in these parts and warrant a stop if you are travelling on the EN 245 to or from Sousel. The surrounding countryside always appears greener than elsewhere due to the ample water from streams like the Vide, Sousel, Almadaye, Avis and Seda. Storks and egrets are plentiful.

Every effort should be made to visit nearby Avis because it was here that the House of Avis started. It ruled Portugal from 1383 to 1580. The castle was built in the first part of the 13th century by a military order from Spain, subsequently known as the Knights of Avis, of which João I was the twentieth Grand Master. He married Philippa of Lancaster in 1387. Although both castle and convent are now sadly neglected, it is not difficult to imagine past glories.

There are now so many pousadas in the Alentejo that one is spoilt for choice. Sousel is centrally located and quiet and its sporting facilities make it a little different.

POUSADA ACTIVITIES

Pool, family games and snooker

AREA ACTIVITIES

Country walks, mountain bikes, horse riding, four-wheel driving, canoeing, shooting (pigeon, grouse, rabbit, hare, partridge and wild boar), falconry shows and archery.

HOW TO FIND

Care needed. Turn west in Sousel on the Cano - Casa Branca road. Almost immediately turn left. Aim for the summit of a prominent nearby hill (3kms).

T his sumptuous pousada is a conversion of the mainly 13th-century royal palace and castle standing within the walled town. It has been a favourite since it opened in 1970. Recent improvements have added a sizeable swimming pool and surrounding terrace.

It was the home of King Dinis (1279-1325) who founded Coimbra University. His wife, Isabel, died here in 1336. So did King Pedro I in 1367. Don't miss the little chapel at the side of the pousada, which occupies the site of the bedroom in which

Queen Isabel is presumed to have spent her last earthly days. Reception will tell you how to get in, for it is not well-publicised. The walls of Capela da Rainha Santa Isabel depict the Queen's life, which she devoted to the poor. When challenged by King Dinis about her generosity to the needy, she opened the folds of her dress. The hidden gold or bread (history is not sure which) had miraculously turned into roses. The Holy Queen was canonized 289 years after her death.

Opposite the chapel is a small but interesting museum and there are two other churches in the square. The great 27-metre tower is known as the Tower of the Three Crowns since its construction spanned the reigns of Sancho II, Afonso III and King Dinis. As with Beja, it is a landmark as one approaches the town.

The accommodation is well laid out. A spacious entrance foyer and reception

> ❝ *this is a place in which to give yourself a royal treat* ❞

H
33

area lead to the drawing-room and bar. Also on this floor is the gigantic dining-room seating 200. It has a fine vaulted ceiling. The well-furnished bedrooms can be reached by a staircase or lift in the entrance hall. There are now 33 bedrooms. The tables in the dining-room are immaculate with good china, glassware and cutlery. The food is as good as befits the setting. It is a restaurant which warrants a little extravagance. Unless you are cheese-paring by nature or by necessity, this is a place in which to give yourself a royal treat - indeed kings have dined here. Wines are no problem, and anything from this area, be it white or red, is a good bet. Nearby Borba's red 'Reserva' is greatly to our liking.

There is a great deal to see in and around Estremoz and, as always, the problem is what to include in a relatively short visit. In the town, have a look at the Misericordia, the city walls and the old town hall in Casa dos Paços. There are a number of marble quarries around nearby Borba, and the Royal Palace of Vila Viçosa (described under the previous two pousadas) should be included in your tour. The handmade carpets of Arraiolos, work in marble, cork, clay, cane and metal are all produced by skilled local craftsmen. It is not difficult to find a little present for the folks back home.

POUSADA ACTIVITIES

Swimming pool and family games.

AREA ACTIVITIES

Shooting, country walks, cycling, theme tours and golf.

HOW TO FIND

Easy. In the town itself, occupying a commanding position, it can be seen from the main road (on your left if you are travelling towards Badajoz and Spain).

66 many memories of a journey fade with time, but Flor da Rosa will remain etched in the mind forever 99

To appreciate Flor da Rosa and nearby Crato, it is helpful to know a little of the history of this ancient area. Stone Age man was resident in these parts. Well-preserved megalithic tombs are proof of this. There is one just short of nearby Aldeia de Mata.

The fortified monastery of Flor da Rosa was founded in 1356 by the first Prior of Crato, Frei Álvaro Gonçalves Pereira. His further claim to fame was the fathering of the Holy Constable, Nun Álvares Pereira, commander of João I's forces who defeated a substantially superior Spanish force at the famous Battle of Aljubarrota in 1385. (*See Pousada Mestre A. Domingues, Batalha*)

The history of the last Prior of Crato is absorbing. Prior Dom António had a tenuous and convoluted claim to the throne when the childless Cardinal King Henrique died in 1580. António claimed he was the illegitimate son of Prince Luis, the brother of former King João III, who died in 1557. Rather than accept the more substantial claim of Philip of Spain, the Portuguese opted for Prior Crato. His reign was short-lived. One day in fact! Not easily deterred, he had another abortive attempt in 1589.

This national monument has been skilfully restored. What was once a ruin is now a pousada incorporating all the comforts of the 21st century whilst at the same time preserving the atmosphere and many of the features of its medieval past.

The first view of Flor da Rosa is impressive. It has the power and yet the

H 24

simplicity to make its mark on the visitor. Many memories of a journey fade with time, but Flor da Rosa will remain acid-etched in the mind forever. The stonework inside and the vaulting of the cloisters are medieval workmanship of a very high standard. The patient and sympathetic skills of modern craftsmen in restoring this important building must have given enormous satisfaction to all concerned. To be super critical, the decor and furnishings are not of the same standard.

The pousada opened in 1995 and has 24 rooms. Eleven are located within the original structure and 13 in an added modern wing overlooking the gardens and a good swimming pool. There is a lift. Of the 11 original bedrooms, three are located in the tower. The Prior is reputed to have slept in one of them. His mortal remains rest in the church adjoining the entrance.

There is much of interest to see in the immediate vicinity of Crato and Alter do Chão, and even more if the sizeable town of Portalegre (23 kms) is included. Crato is a prosperous agricultural town best explored on foot. The library is housed in the original prison (18th-century), and older buildings include what is left of the Palácio of the Priores of Crato, the castle and the 16th-century parish church. The charm of Crato lies not only in its monuments, but in smaller private houses which have considerable personality.

The Romans knew how to build well and the bridge across the river near Sede is proof of it. You will go over it if taking the Ponte de Sor road. Whatever route you take on leaving Flor da Rosa, the betting is you will return.

POUSADA ACTIVITIES

Swimming pool, snooker and family games.

AREA ACTIVITIES

Shooting, fishing, golf, horse riding, falconry shows and carriage tours.

HOW TO FIND

Easy. The Flor da Rosa pousada is situated in the village of the same name 2kms from Crato on the road to Alpalhão.

A s has been mentioned in the introduction to the Upper Alentejo, Arraiolos is famous for its carpets. It is a cottage industry probably dating from the time of the Moorish occupation. The designs reflect their ancient origin. Early carpets included floral, plant and tree motifs, followed in later work by the

increasing inclusion of animals and birds. It is a thriving industry carried on with the same basic designs and in the same traditional way that has satisfied both manufacturer and customer over the centuries.

Not only are Arraiolos carpets a pleasure to look at (they are often used as wall decorations), they have proved a fine investment. A carpet bought 15 years ago would have increased in value sixfold.

Modern technology is supplementing rather than changing the original design

POUSADA DE ARRAIOLOS

Nossa Sra. da Assunção

H 32

methods which hitherto have been traced by hand using paper templates. Recently, a 18m x 7m carpet made for the prestigious Lisbon offices of Banco Comercial Português was produced by hand in the traditional way, but the design was computer assisted.

In the village there are several manufacturers where you can see work being carried out and there is a permanent exhibition of the craft in the town hall.

The town is pleasant enough. It stands on a hill dominated by the ruins of its 14th-century castle. Increasingly, the shops and houses are geared to the tourist and carpet trade, but this does not detract from the rural atmosphere of the tiny town.

The pousada lies a little to the north of the town in the Valley of the Flowers and is a conversion of the Convento dos Lóios. It was opened late in 1996 and the architect José Paulo dos Santos has been able to maintain the very high standards set in recent conversions of ancient monuments. Certainly with its

POUSADA ACTIVITIES

Swimming pool, tennis, family games and horse riding.

AREA ACTIVITIES

Shooting (rabbit, grouse, hare and partridge), countryside bicycle tours, horse riding, four-wheel driving, hot air ballooning, canoeing, paintball, traditional games and karting.

HOW TO FIND

Easy. Arraiolos is halfway between Estremoz and Montemor o Novo. The pousada is 200m from Arraiolos, going in the direction of Pavia.

attractive cloisters, old tiling and an interesting mélange of Moorish and Manueline styles, it has everything going for it.

Overlooked by the early 14th century castle, this charming pousada was originally Conde (Count) Álvaro Pires de Castro's house, which was subsequently replaced by the convent. Álvaro was the brother of the charmer Inês de Castro, King Pedro's mistress. She pre-deceased him and her story is told in the chapter on the pousada S. Domingos at Batalha. In brief, she was exhumed, her corpse crowned and court officials ordered to pay homage to their new queen!

The monastery, dedicated to Nossa Senhora da Assunção, was started in 1527. Its founder, João Garcês, is buried in the side chapel of the convent's church. Do, please, have a look at this beautifully restored church with its handsome *azulejos* (painted glazed tiles). It is on the right of the entrance. With the extinction of religious orders in the 19th century the secularised property was sold by the state to the Corte Real family, whose most famous son, Miguel, many believe was the first European to set foot on mainland America. In more recent times the state repurchased the property from the descendents of the Corte Real family and has done a wonderful job in restoring and opening the building as a de luxe pousada.

There is much for the energetic to do in and around the pousada. Tennis, riding and swimming are all provided, including a pool for the children.

Whilst in the area, have a look at the unique Megalithic tomb at Pavia (15 kms). It has a minute Christian chapel inside. The fountain of Almocreves on the outskirts is typically Portuguese and although we have not yet visited the Solar da Sempre

Noiva, it sounds as though it would be worth the journey. It is just south of the town (4 kms), off the Évora road. Reputedly it was the home of Juliana de Sousa Coutinho. Because of her unwillingness to marry, she became known, as the house is today, as Sempre Noiva (always the fiancée).

There is a good example of an early fortified manor-house on the outskirts of Brotas (30 kms). It is known as the Tower of the Eagles (Torre das Águias).

With the opening of more and more pousadas in Alentejo, the competition must be good for the traveller. Whether you enjoy the sporting amenities or prefer to watch others from the comfort of your bedroom balcony, we would be astounded if you did not leave with regret and with long-lasting memories of this exceptional pousada.

" a top category pousada ...
the bedrooms are conversions
from the original monastic cells "

A top category pousada opened in 1965, the Dos Lóios or St Eligius Monastery was consecrated to St John the Evangelist in 1491. To this day the eagle emblem of St John remains in the coat of arms. Just as the Lóios monks in their sky blue robes dispensed hospitality and charity in the 15th century, so today on the same site this unique pousada offers the traveller a similar warmth of welcome.

The cloisters have been glassed in to form a dining-room which retains its Manueline architecture and horseshoe arches, its vaulted ceiling and marble font. A meal in these surroundings, overlooking the central courtyard, is an experience which will long remain in the memory.

The bedrooms are conversions from the original monastic cells. The furnishings throughout are in good taste and in keeping with this lovely building. There is a suite with an impressive baroque antechamber and if many of the Lisbon hotels warrant five stars, Dos Lóios warrants ten!

H

32

The swimming pool may not be of Olympic proportions, but it is very inviting after a day's drive or sightseeing.

Évora, the capital of the Alentejo, is to be savoured rather than gobbled. It is a town of arches, arcades, aqueducts, *azulejos* and academics. It has had a flourishing university since the 15th and 16th centuries when it was the centre of court life. It is outside the scope of this book to give a detailed account of what to see in the town. The local tourist office will provide a suggested itinerary and the better guide books devote several pages to the subject.

The Roman Temple of Diana is on your doorstep. It was excavated in 1870 having previously been used as a slaughterhouse. If you have neither time nor inclination to explore the town in detail, you should certainly take a look at Praça do Geraldo with its arcaded and shady pavements. Casa Cordovil in Largo de Moura clearly shows Arab influence on Portuguese architecture. In the older parts of the city, around Rua da Alcárcova (Ditch Street), you will find - with the aid of your dictionary - the streets of the 'Countess's tailor', the 'Cardinal's nurses', the 'Lisping man' and even the 'Unshaven man'. The Chapel of Bones, adjoining São Francisco church, is a salutary reminder of our own mortality, confirmed by an inspection of the megalithic remains at Almindres (12 kms west). More cheering are the colourful carpets of Arraiolos (20 kms). There is much to see in this ancient part of Portugal and you need only a short stroll from the pousada to rub shoulders with the past.

POUSADA ACTIVITIES

Pool and family games.

AREA ACTIVITIES

Shooting (all varieties), cultural tours or city, mountain bike tours, four-wheel driving, hot air ballooning, horse riding, shooting range and karting.

HOW TO FIND

Very easy. In the centre of the town facing the famous remains of the Temple of Diana.

The one thing Portugal is not short of is palaces. Near Lisbon, Ajuda and Queluz and the palaces of Sintra are a joy. Here at Vila Viçosa is the great Ducal Palace of the Bragança family who ruled Portugal from the middle of the 17th century to the end of the monarchy in 1910.

The present Duke of Bragança, D. Duarte, pretender to the Portuguese throne, married at Jerónimos Monastery in Lisbon in 1995, an occasion to which the media did full justice and which sparked a fire of enthusiasm among a minority for the return of the monarchy. It happened in Spain, but a repetition in Portugal is most improbable. Nevertheless, the link with the past is strong and much loved by the romantic nature of the Portuguese. Nowhere is this past link more clearly defined than in the Palace at Vila Viçosa. Manuel II, the last king and ancestor of D. Duarte, spent his last days in Portugal here before going into exile in England. Surrounded by his beloved books, he died the day after watching the tennis at Wimbledon in 1932. Catherine of Bragança, who married King Charles II of England, was born at Vila Viçosa in 1638.

The palace, which was begun in 1501 and finished mainly in the 17th century, became the main residence of the Braganças and now houses an interesting

> *it is good to see these treasures of Portugal being restored and put to practical use*

collection of family memorabilia. It dominates a spacious square in which a statue of the first Bragança king, João IV, sits astride his charger. The classical facade of 100 metres has a powerful monotony.

Hitherto, visitors to the palace (which is open to the public) often stayed at the nearby Elvas or Estremoz pousadas. They do not have to travel even that distance with the opening of the D. João IV pousada.

Adjoining the palace, on the south side of the square, is the Convento das Chagas de Cristo (1532) and it is here that the new pousada has been constructed. A delightful building architecturally, with rather sombre connotations as it was the final resting place of several former duchesses. With some good tiling and attractive cloisters, it has been converted into a well-run modern pousada. It is good to see these treasures of Portugal being restored and put to practical use.

It is an area which takes an above average interest in food - the palace was surrounded by acres of hunting country in the days of the Braganças. The cuisine lives up to past reputation and the wines of Borba (5 kms) are among the best that Alentejo, if not Portugal, has to offer.

POUSADA ACTIVITIES

Swimming pool, family games and snooker.

AREA ACTIVITIES

Countryside walking excursions and hot air ballooning.

HOW TO FIND

Easy. From Estremoz, take the road to Borba. 5kms from Borba you will arrive at Vila Viçosa. The pousada is situated at the entrance of the village on the right side, next to the Ducal Palace.

With an area of 9,079 sq. miles (23,514 sq. km), the Alentejo is by far the largest of the Portuguese provinces. It now has sixteen pousadas. For this reason we have divided the Alentejo into two sections - Upper and Lower.

Some of the highest temperatures, quite often 40°C, are recorded in these parts. This makes an air-conditioned car a pleasurable extravagance if you propose touring the area in the summer months. Many favour the spring or autumn for touring.

It is only in the latter part of this decade that the Alentejo has become a popular holiday venue. It is far more the authentic Portugal than the beaches of the Algarve and Estremadura. It gets its name from *alem Tejo* (beyond the Tagus). With improved irrigation from man-made dams it increasingly provides Portugal's cereal crops. It is a prolific cork-producing area and the wealth of this once poor province is supplemented by the production of olive oil, rice, salt, marble and some very good wines. Dairy herds and great flocks of sheep roam the open countryside, often with a single person in charge. Frequently dressed in a cape-like *pelico*, the local shepherd resembles a Sherlock Holmes in search of clues. Even if there are giant pig and chicken farming industries, it is as a history-producing region that the Alentejo is best remembered by the visitor.

The fortress towns of places like Beja and the fortified castles of Alvito and Alcácer do Sal constantly remind us of the battlefields of the past. It was here that there was constant intrigue and dispute with the Spanish as to who owned what. It is,

The Province of Lower Alentejo

> *essentially a farming area, it is as a history-producing region that the Alentejo is best remembered by the visitor*

Top: Ruins at Montemor
Centre: Thatched house
in the Sado Estuary
Below: Sines

however, to the occupation of the Romans, and particularly the 500-year stay of the Moors, that the Alentejo owes much of its character. There are several museums in which you can see artefacts from the past, and the ruins near the wine-growing area of Vidigueira, Miróbriga on the outskirts of Santiago do Cacém, and Pisões, south of Beja, are powerful reminders of the Roman occupation. The Moorish influence is ever

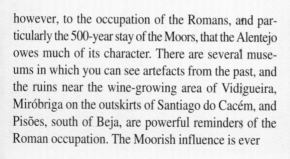

present and is startlingly evident in the architecture of Mértola, Moura and Serpa.

As we have seen, the Alentejo is essentially a farming area, but there are craftsmen in metal and wood, whose skills are often on display in local markets, side streets and on the roadside. The manufacture of *chocalhos* (not to be confused with chocolates) can be seen in the village of Alcáçovas where Senhor João Penetra has a collection of nearly 1,000 of these cowbells, often artistically engraved. In various sizes, they make fascinating regional souvenirs and are now made in a number of towns, including Serpa.

You may not be a Hemingway and bullfighting may not be your idea of a Saturday afternoon sport, but places like Alcácer do Sal, away from tourist commercialisation, produce *corridas*

of authenticity and atmosphere.

In spring, when the great pasturelands and meadows of the Alentejo are streaked with colourful ribbons of wild flowers, there is no more interesting province to tour. To be able to do so with a choice of comfortable and interesting pousada accommodation increasingly makes the area a must for the inquisitive traveller.

Opposite top: S. Domingos lake.
Opposite centre: Serpa
Opposite bottom: Mértola church
Top left: Porto Covo
Top right: Hilltop front near S. Domingos
Below: Roman ruins at Vila de Frades

Alcácer do Sal used to take a vast volume of traffic travelling across its reinforced bridge. A bypass to the west has greatly improved the north/south journey to and from Lisbon and has restored some tranquillity to this attractive hillside town overlooking the quiet waters of the river Sado. Whether the shopkeepers and restaurant owners are overjoyed with the improved traffic conditions is another matter. Perhaps the pousada will do something to restore passing trade.

Alcácer do Sal was conquered by many different peoples: before the Roman occupation it was called Eviom and had trade with the Mediterranean countries; the Romans called it Salata Urbs Imperatoria; it was capital city of the Visigothic municipality; it was dominated by the Arabs at the end of the 8th century, becoming one of the most important trade cities in the peninsula; it was conquered by the Vikings at the end of the 10th century; D. Afonso Henriques, the first king of Portugal, tried to conquer it in 1158, but it only became a Portuguese village in 1217 with King Afonso II. In 1500, the castle built by the Arabs had no military purpose any longer, and so became a Carmelita de Aracelli convent during the 16th century.

The European Union helped ENATUR fund the restoration of Alcácer do Sal's castle, which has been a listed national monument since 1916. The resulting pousada, which opened in March 1998, has 35 bedrooms, public rooms, a swimming pool and gardens. During excavations, ruins of a Roman temple and a Moslem mosque were unearthed and artefacts are displayed in the remodelled building for the interest of guests.

Ornithologists will be comforted to learn that even bureaucrats have compassion for our feathered friends. Temporary nesting has been provided for the displaced storks who have made the castle their home for many years. No doubt this was

> **"** *nesting has been provided for displaced storks who have made the castle their home for many years* **"**

H

35

POUSADA ACTIVITIES

Swimming pool.

AREA ACTIVITIES

Shooting, fishing, golf, water sports, canoeing, cruises, country walks, cycling, theme tours, horse riding, four-wheel driving, hot air ballooning, paintball, family games, archery, cross bow, bird watching and diving.

HOW TO FIND

Very easy. The pousada is in the Castle within the town of Alcácer do Sal. Just follow the signs to the Castle and the Pousada.

allowed for in the 1,600,000,000 escudos estimated to carry out the total work.

At one time this was a prolific salt-producing area (*sal* is the Portuguese word for salt), but now the salt flats have been replaced with rice fields.

Troia, on the coast, and Grândola are within exploring distance.

The completion of D. Afonso II is certainly to the benefit of the traveller, and adds to the magnificent choice of pousadas in the Alentejo.

SETÚBAL
Pinheiro
A2 Santa Susana
IP1
Barragem
EN 253 Pego do Altar
Comporta ALCÁCER DO SAL
Torrão
Barragem
Vale do Gaio

This small pousada is on a lakeside and has an intimate welcoming atmosphere. Like the pousada further south at Santa Clara-a-Velha, it is a conversion of the house of the chief engineer who supervised the building of the Barragem de Trigo de Morais, more commonly know as Vale do Gaio. The *barragem*, or reservoir, was formed by the damming of the River Sado and its tributaries. The pousada was opened in 1977. It had become rather rundown and seedy before it was closed in 1995 for a much needed, major modernisation. It reopened at the end of 1996 with extra bedrooms and completely refurbished.

Peace is here in abundance. The gentle views across the lake from the terrace, the early morning viridian colouring, particularly in the spring, and the rise of a fish breaking the still waters are all part of this tranquil scene. It may not be as spectacular as Santa Clara, but what it lacks in grandeur is more than compensated for by its private, secluded charm and a feeling that the whole picture was painted especially for you.

This is excellent walking country and a paradise for dogs. Fir trees growing in

POUSADA DE TORRÃO

Vale do Gaio

R 14

POUSADA ACTIVITIES

Swimming pool, family games, carriage tours, cruises and rowing.

AREA ACTIVITIES

Shooting, fishing (dam), countryside bicycle excursions, cruises, four-wheel driving, hot air ballooning, canoeing and archery.

HOW TO FIND

Not easy. Take the Beja road out of Alcácer do Sal. After about 27 kms - about 8 kms from Torrão - a road on the right (marked "Pousada") takes off at a right angle. Drive on through the woods for about 4 kms.

the vicinity are tapped for their resin. You are surrounded by acres of cork oak, eucalyptus and paddy fields which were originally salt-flats. The water attracts bird-life and a pair of binoculars is useful. Fishing, swimming in the lake and rough shooting are all available. There are also a couple of dinghies if you fancy a row on the lake.

The ancient town of Alcácer do Sal (the castle of salt) is 30 kms to the west. It is an interesting riverside town overlooking the Sado which winds its tortuous way to the sea at Setúbal. Like a dog, it seems to sniff its way along without any preconceived ideas of where it is going.

If you would like to see a bullfight, there is a bullring on the outskirts of the town where you will get the authentic atmosphere, for this is the home of country folk rather than tourism. Remember, in Portugal the bull is not killed in the ring, but merely wrestled to a standstill by a team of *forcados*.

Despite the new pousada of D. Afonso II in the castle of Alcácer do Sal, Vale do Gaio will retain its admirers. It is a joy at any time of the year. The winter is a favourite for many. After the searing heat of the summer, walking is a pleasure and a roaring log fire at the end of the day is difficult to leave. If you want to 'get away from it all', the Valley of the Jays is the place. To the east of the pousada, Torrão (8 kms) is pleasant without being exceptional. Make the effort to drive another 12 kms to Alcáçovas. King Dinis, known as 'the farmer monarch' (1279-1325), had a palace built here. Other noblemen followed. The palaces of the Condes das Alcáçovas and the Barahonas are close to the centre.

" *a top grade pousada...*
a brace of peacocks strut
disdainfully among the guests **"**

The castle of Alvito was opened as a top grade pousada at the end of 1993. As you enjoy a drink in the courtyard, it is interesting to reflect on its history. In 1482, King Afonso V gave permission for the second Baron and Lord of Alvito to build a castle here. Before he was created baron, Sr João da Silveira had held many government posts, including secretary of state and inspector of the treasury. At that time it was unique for a private individual to own a castle: they

were in royal ownership. Through the centuries many kings and queens of Portugal have stayed here. It was a place of importance and prestige, but by the end of the 19th century the castle was abandoned and became the home of gypsy squatters. Fortunately, the House of Bragança Foundation rescued the castle from further neglect and subsequently granted a lease for an initial period of 25 years for the conversion to the pousada we know today. The architect has done a good job, combining all the modern accoutrements without detracting from the ambience of the past.

There are 20 bedrooms, lifts, reception rooms and a dining-room seating 100. Outside, there is a garden with a swimming pool and a little amphitheatre. A brace of peacocks strut disdainfully among the guests.

POUSADA DE ALVITO

Castelo de Alvito

H 20

We are close to Vidigueira, a major wine-producing region. If you take the N258, it is about 25 kms and you can inspect the main production plant. En route, look in at the Roman manor house. At one time it was the property of the great sailor Vasco da Gama. Now a national monument, S. Cacufate was ransacked and even dynamited in order to obtain brickwork for other buildings.

Close at hand is Paço de Agua de Peixes (6kms). As the name suggests, there is abundant water from a prolific underground source which has been pouring into fountains and ornamental ponds for centuries. The property is privately owned and not open to the public unless you are lucky enough to persuade the caretaker to show you around. We had no difficulty in wandering through the gardens and enjoying the shade of the trees overhanging the ornamental waters that run the full length of the rear facade. This 15th-century manor house is an oasis in the plains and it is hoped that sufficient funds will be made available to preserve the deteriorating structure. The architecture is a mishmash of Moorish, Manueline and Gothic.

Drive your car in any direction and you will discover a way of life that has moved into the 21st century with reluctance. Local craftsmen are particularly adept with wood. In nearby Cuba, Café Central in Rua Serpa Pinto has a montage of every conceivable farm instrument beautifully executed to scale.

After a stay at Castelo de Alvito, however short, you will have absorbed some of the unique atmosphere of the Alentejo - a lonely, vast, hot, but very seductive province.

POUSADA ACTIVITIES

Swimming pool, family games and snooker.

AREA ACTIVITIES

Shooting (rabbits, hares and partridges), canoeing, horse riding, country walks and bicycle tours.

HOW TO FIND
Easy. In the centre of this small country town.

143

This early pousada, opened in 1947, is nowadays far less a staging post en route to Lisbon than a tourist centre from which to explore the west coast. Creeper-clad and situated on the outskirts of the town, it resembles a small country house. The grounds are well-wooded and screen the nearby road and traffic noise. Considerable work has recently been undertaken to modernise and refurbish the buildings. The swimming pool and the adjoining wisteria-clad terrace have also been improved.

Before moving on, have a look at the castle and church erected on a Moorish site by the Knights Templar. They give a good viewing point. Within walking distance of the pousada (1.5 km) are the Roman ruins of Mirobriga.

If you approach Santiago do Cacém from the south, the barren scenery of the Sagres peninsular improves after Vila do Bispo. Eucalyptus trees line the route, a pine forest comes into view; the land is cultivated and productively green. On the high ground a windmill dominates the skyline and a donkey plods homewards with a load which would intimidate many forms of mechanical transport.

> *creeper-clad and situated on the outskirts of town, it resembles a small country house*

R

8

POUSADA ACTIVITIES

Swimming pool and family games

AREA ACTIVITIES

Shooting (rabbit and hare), fishing (sea and dam), windsurfing, surfing, bike tours, cruises, four-wheel driving, four-wheel motorbikes, carriage tours, horse riding (school), bird watching and paintball.

HOW TO FIND
Fairly easy. Santiago do Cacém, lies 17kms from Sines at the junction of the roads from Grândola and Beja. The pousada is on the outskirts of the town, on the road from Grândola, on the left, opposite a garage/filling station.

Along this west coast are numerous magnificent beaches, not so well-known as those along the Algarve's southern coastline, but nonetheless among the best in Europe. They are popular with the Portuguese and, being nearer Lisbon, are fairly crowded in summer, particularly in August. There are so many of them and they are so vast that a quiet spot is not difficult to find. Take care, however, to observe elementary swimming precautions. Do not swim on an outgoing tide or when it is rough, and observe the flags and instructions of the lifeguards.

Near the pousada there are two inland lagoons, one at Santo André where you can relax and enjoy a good eel stew. Further south and on the other side of Sines, Porto Covo should be put on your itinerary. Not far offshore is the fortress island of Pessegueiro with its air of mystery and intrigue. The locals fish off the rocks in rafts which look as though they were the forerunners of Kon-Tiki. Further south is the equally attractive Vila Nova de Milfontes where, on either side of the mouth of the River Mira, there are good sandy beaches. Odemira and Ourique are small towns, pleasant enough but not worth a special visit.

Since 1971, Sines (17 kms) has become an increasingly commercialised port. It is now a major tanker-terminal. Surrounding the town, the birthplace of Vasco da Gama, huge refineries house the country's strategic oil reserves. This necessary development has done little to increase the touristic appeal of the town, but it has improved the road network.

T his *quinta* (farm) was acquired in 1991 largely to provide overflow accommodation for the very busy and heavily booked São Tiago pousada in the town. It has quickly established itself as a pousada in its own right. Many prefer the peacefulness of this country estate, which is only 5 kms from Santiago do Cacém.

It is rather difficult to find. Take the Sines road from near the pousada in town. 5 km along this road, turn right on to a minor road. There is a sign, but it is largely obscured by another one. Go through the tunnel which runs beneath the main road you have just left. At the T-junction turn left and you will find the tree-lined drive to the *quinta* about   100 metres on your right.

Quinta da Ortiga stands in its own grounds of four hectares (10 acres) and is surrounded by farming land. Its 13 bedrooms are much in demand, particularly at weekends. The pool area and terraces are a delight. The pool is a redesigned modernisation of the original belonging to the *quinta*.

There is a very adequate wine list and the advice of the staff is worth taking.

In the grounds, a tiny chapel reminds the visitor that generations of previous owners have worshipped here. There is a riding stable and plans

> *many prefer the peacefulness of this country estate, which is much in demand, particularly at weekends*

Quinta da Ortiga

R
13

POUSADA ACTIVITIES

Swimming pool and family games.

AREA ACTIVITIES

Shooting (rabbit and hare), fishing (sea and dam), windsurfing, surfing, bicycle tours, cruises, four-wheel driving, four-wheel motorbikes, carriage tours, donkey cart tours, horse riding (school), bird watching and paintball.

HOW TO FIND
Tricky. Off the Santiago - Sines road. See text.

for a tennis court may have fructified by the time you stay.

In view of its proximity to the São Tiago pousada, much that has been written under that chapter applies equally to the Quinta da Ortiga pousada. We recommend this pousada to travellers who enjoy an isolated country house atmosphere, with good amenities and value for money.

Within three hours drive south of Lisbon, this pousada was opened in 1971. The building was originally the office and home of the chief engineer in charge of the construction of the Santa Clara *barragem*. A vast artificial lake formed by damming the River Mira and its tributaries, it now brings much needed water to the farmlands of the Lower Alentejo. Today, the former office provides the perfect position to overlook the sheltered waters which are 44 kms long and 90 metres deep.

It is a wonderfully peaceful scene, with the waters enclosed by slopes of fir and eucalyptus. Sailing, swimming, fishing, walking and duck shooting are available sports - the first four without formality, although a licence is required from Odemira for shooting. The summer attracts a lot of campers. The local authority has restricted their occupation to certain areas as their spread around the entire perimeter did little to enhance the scenic and peaceful charm of the lake.

> *the perfect position overlooking sheltered waters enclosed by slopes of fir and eucalyptus*

R

19

The pousada was out of commission for over a year while extensive modernisation and improvements were being carried out. It reopened in 1996. We were among the early visitors and were very impressed with the transformation that had taken place. Of course the setting and view were always there, but the prolific winter rains had increased the level of the lake and enhanced the outlook - if that was possible. A suite and extra bedrooms have been added. There is now a swimming pool with separate children's pool and playground, as well as enlarged and redesigned reception rooms. The standard of finish is exceptionally high. The woodwork and marble outclass many of the other pousadas.

The nearby village is pleasant, but unexciting. Many of the street names (India, Goa, Dom Henriques) remind the traveller of Portugal's great past.

Take the opportunity of travelling south through the Serra de Monchique to Monchique itself (33 km). This marvellous mountain scenery is perhaps better enjoyed by passengers than the driver, who has his work cut out negotiating innumerable twists and turns. On either side, the land sweeps away in great ranges of fir, eucalyptus and cork. The bark is stripped from cork trees every nine years and Nave Redonda, which you pass, is a collecting centre for this valuable product. There are plenty of partridge in this sparsely populated mountain range and you may be lucky enough to see a mongoose.

You will not regret a visit to or stay at Santa Clara. It has everything, including bicycles and boats for hire if you are energetic. For many, the tranquil view from the terraces and the excellent accommodation, wines and food are, in themselves, sufficient raison d'être.

POUSADA ACTIVITIES
Swimming pool, fishing, countryside bycicle excursions and cruises (motorboat and rowboat).

AREA ACTIVITIES
Canoeing (river), horse riding, four-wheel driving and bird watching.

HOW TO FIND
Needs care. 21kms from Odemira on the Ourique road you come to Odemira railway station and the junction of the road going south to Santa Clara-a-Velha. Go past the town and take the first proper road on your left; this leads, after 4kms, to the pousada.

The architects made a splendid job of converting a 13th-century monastery into this pousada, opened in 1994. As a centrally-located building it had rather a chequered career before ENATUR took on the task of transforming it into a top grade hotel. It served as an army barracks in the mid-19th century and more recently as a discotheque, but despite these vicissitudes it has emerged as an integral part of this ancient market town.

The oldest parts of the converted building are the little chapel, the adjoining cloisters and the chapter house, which date from the 13th and 14th centuries. Much of the rest, including the impressive church, date from the 17th century. Today, this ancient building is a very beautiful, spacious and comfortable pousada with 35 rooms, drawing-rooms, music room, bar, a swimming pool, tennis court, terrace, maturing gardens and ample space for conferences and exhibitions.

It is all too easy in the comfort of São Francisco and its grounds not to venture too far from base. It would be a pity not to give Beja the once over. It is an

> *"today this ancient building is a very beautiful, spacious and comfortable pousada"*

H 35

POUSADA ACTIVITIES

Swimming pool, tennis court, snooker and family games.

AREA ACTIVITIES

Shooting, fishing, horse riding, country walks, cruises, four-wheel driving, carriage drives, theme tours, water sports (river and dam), hot air ballooning, micro lighting, bird watching, paintball, archery and cross bow.

HOW TO FIND

Very easy. The pousada is situated in the centre of Beja next to the police station (PSP). Whichever direction you are coming from, enter the city and at about 3kms you will find directions to the pousada.

attractive and historic town. Many streets are shaded by orange trees and the town centre is restricted to pedestrians. It is a wealthy area and many of the most exclusive shops are located in secondary streets. To find them, we suggest a journey on foot to the Convento of Nossa Senhora da Conceição which houses the Rainha D. Leonor Museum with its fine *azulejos* and leather-bound prayer books.

The romantic among you may be intrigued by the goings-on of Sister Mariana Alcoforado. She, perhaps ill-advisedly, committed her romance with a French colonel to paper. The letters, published in French in 1669, did not greatly enhance the harmony within the colonel's family (Marquis de Saint-Lèger), nor did they do a lot for the tranquillity and serenity of the holy Order of Saint Clara. The window at which they reputedly arranged their trysts is at the end of the first floor corridor.

The same admission ticket entitles the bearer to visit the Church of Santo Amaro. A little location map is provided. On the way there are some quite classy boutiques and perfumeries. If you are energetic and have a good head for heights, 200 steps bring the intrepid to the summit of the castle tower, which also houses a military museum.

Leaving Beja on the N18 to Aljustrel, there is a Roman site at Pisões (7 kms). This is a reminder of the influence brought to these parts by the Romans.

The pousada de São Francisco provides the ideal setting to contemplate the past in the comfort of the present.

B uilt in the early 1970's, the pousada stands on high and commanding ground with immense views across the plains of Alentejo to the Sierra de Andevalo in Spain. Money has been spent on improvements and a swimming pool has been added to refresh tired limbs after a day's travelling. Although modern, the bedrooms are spacious with balconies offering fantastic views. There is also a fine terrace adjoining the dining-room and lounge.

The town itself has seen more prosperous days. The British-financed copper mine at Mina de S. Domingos to the south used to employ 7,000 people and bring a lot of business. It closed about 30 years ago. Serpa now is a restful, gentle town best explored on foot. Have a look at the mellowed aqueduct, the church, the 14th-century clock tower and the castle destroyed and rebuilt so many times in the turbulent past of this walled city. Don't rush to leave Serpa. The longer you stay the more you will find: craftsmen working in metal, wood, cork and horn; shady squares, wrought-iron balconies, fountains, chimneys, watermill, and wells, all reflecting the influence of Romans

> ❝ *the bedrooms are spacious with balconies offering fantastic views... don't rush to leave Serpa* ❞

R

18

and Moors whose home this was.

You will pack your bags with reluctance. Before you do, have a peep at the tiny chapel adjoining the car park. Capela de Nossa Senhora de Guadalupe is probably 14th-century, although the custodian claims it to be 9th-century. It has more letters in its name than it has seats, and it has a survey beacon as part of its structure.

Of course it is impossible in a relatively short tour to see everything, but if you can, make time to look at Moura and the northern road from there to Barrancos on the Spanish border. This is the most easterly part of Portugal and the lonely, ruined castle at Noudar, built by King Afonso in 1346, recaptures the tumultuous past far better than any history book.

POUSADA ACTIVITIES

Swimming pool and family games.

AREA ACTIVITIES

Shooting and horse riding.

HOW TO FIND

Fairly easy. Take the road out of Serpa and travel towards the frontier with Spain. After about 3kms you will see the pousada on your right, standing on a hill, up a small track.